ANTIQUES AND THEIR VALUES

SILVER 1650 ~ 1800

COMPILED BY TONY CURTIS

While every care has been taken in the compiling of information contained in this volume the publishers cannot accept any liability for loss, financial or otherwise, incurred by reliance placed on the information herein.

All prices quoted in this book are obtained from a variety of auctions in various countries and are converted to dollars at the rate of exchange prevalent at the time of sale.

ISBN 0-86248-016-7

Copyright © Lyle Publications MCMLXXXI
Published by Lyle Publications, Glenmayne, Galashiels, Selkirkshire, Scotland.

INTRODUCTION

This book is one of a series specially devised to aid the busy professional dealer in his everyday trading. It will also prove to be of great value to all collectors and those with goods to sell, for it is crammed with illustrations, brief descriptions and valuations of hundreds of antiques.

Every effort has been made to ensure that each specialised volume contains the widest possible variety of goods in its particular category though the greatest emphasis is placed on the middle bracket of trade goods rather than on those once-in-a-lifetime museum pieces whose values are of academic rather than practical interest to the vast majority of dealers and collectors.

This policy has been followed as a direct consequence of requests from dealers who sensibly realise that, no matter how comprehensive their knowledge, there is always a need for reliable, up-to-date reference works for identification and valuation purposes.

When using your Antiques and their Values Book to assess the worth of goods, please bear in mind that it would be impossible to place upon any item a precise value which would hold good under all circumstances. No antique has an exactly calculable value; its price is always the result of a compromise reached between buyer and seller, and questions of condition, local demand and the business acumen of the parties involved in a sale are all factors which affect the assessment of an object's 'worth' in terms of hard cash.

In the final analysis, however, such factors cancel out when large numbers of sales are taken into account by an experienced valuer, and it is possible to arrive at a surprisingly accurate assessment of current values of antiques; an assessment which may be taken confidently to be a fair indication of the worth of an object and which provides a reliable basis for negotiation.

Throughout this book, objects are grouped under category headings and, to expedite reference, they progress in price order within their own categories. Where the description states 'one of a pair' the value given is that for the pair sold as such.

The publishers wish to express their sincere thanks
to the following for their kind help and assistance
in the production of this volume:

JANICE MONCRIEFF
NICOLA PARK
CARMEN MILIVOYEVICH
ELAINE HARLAND
MAY MUTCH
MARGOT RUTHERFORD
JENNIFER KNOX

Printed by Apollo Press, Worthing, Sussex, England.
Bound by R. J. Acford, Chichester, Sussex, England.

CONTENTS

George III oval shaped cake basket, 14¾in. wide, by Chawner & Emes, London, 1796, 21oz.11dwt.

$810 £360

George III shaped oval cake basket by Alexander Gairdner, Edinburgh, 1778, 14in. wide, 26oz.17dwt.

$1,170 £520

George III silver cake basket by Wm. Tuite, London, 1773, 14in., 19½oz.

$1,240 £550

George III oval cake basket, 1783, by Henry Tudor and Thos. Leader, Sheffield, 20oz.19dwt.$1,350 £600

George III oval cake basket, 12½in. wide, by Richard Morton & Co., Sheffield, 1777, 23oz. 8dwt. $1,485 £660

George III oval shaped cake basket, 13¾in. wide, by H. Bailey, London, 32oz.9dwt.

$1,835 £815

George III oval cake basket, 11¾in. wide, by Richard Morton & Co., Sheffield, 1777, 24oz.3dwt.

$2,025 £900

George III oval cake basket by Chas. Aldridge and Henry Green, London, 1770, 13½in. long, 26oz. 8dwt. $2,365 £1,050

George III oval shaped cake basket by Robt. Hennell, London, 1790, 27oz.16dwt., 14¼in. wide.$2,835 £1,260

George III shaped oval cake basket by Emick Romer, 1767, 26oz., 14¼in. long.   **$2,925 £1,300**

Early George III oval cake basket by Wm. Plummer, London, 1768, 36oz.18dwt., 14¾in. wide.   **$3,220 £1,430**

George II oval shaped cake basket by Elizabeth Godfrey, London, 1743, 13¼in. wide, 57oz.6dwt.   **$4,050 £1,800**

George II shaped oval cake basket by S. Herbert & Co., 1752, 14in. long, 57oz.   **$5,175 £2,300**

George II cake basket by James Schruder, London, 1742, 12¾in. wide, 55oz. 9dwt.   **$6,190 £2,750**

George II shaped oval cake basket, by George Wickes, London, 1740, 13¼in. wide, 61oz.2dwt. **$6,750 £3,000**

George II oval cake basket, 13in. wide, by James Schruder, London, 1738, 51oz,5dwt. **$7,315 £3,250**

George II shaped oval cake basket by Edward Wakelin, London, 1752, 15in. wide, 58oz.8dwt. **$11,250 £5,000**

A fine pierced silver cake basket by Paul de Lamerie, 1731. **£65,250 £29,000**

BASKETS
SUGAR

George III swing-handled sugar basket, circa 1765, 10cm. high. $225 £100

Small George III pierced silver basket by Robt. Hennell, 1787, 4oz. $765 £340

George III swing-handled sugar basket, by Thomas Daniel, 1779.$765 £340

Small George III basket by Hester Bateman, London, 1789, 3in. wide. $765 £340

George III boat-shaped sugar basket, London, 1790, 5oz. $810 £360

Silver sugar basket by Peter and Anne Bateman, 4½oz. $925 £410

SWEETMEAT

George III sweetmeat basket, 4¾in. wide, by Henry Chawner, London, 1795, 5oz.8dwt. $520 £230

George III octagonal silver footed sweetmeat basket, London, 1794, by Robt. Hennell. $610 £270

George III boat-shaped silver sweetmeat basket by Peter Podie, London, 1792, 6½oz. $665 £295

George III boat-shaped sweetmeat basket, 6in. wide, by Henry Chawner, London, 1791, 8oz.3dwt. $675 £300

Silver George III sweetmeat basket, 6in. wide, by Chas. Chesterman, 1784, London, 8oz. 4dwt. $675 £300

George III boat-shaped silver sweetmeat basket, by Peter, Anne and William Bateman. $730 £325

George III silver gilt metal oval sweetmeat basket, 6¾in. wide, by Vere & Lutwyche, London, 1767, 6oz.5dwt. $945 £420

Fine silver sweetmeat basket by William Vincent, London, 1786, 6in. wide, 8oz.10dwt. $1,015 £450

George III boat-shaped sweetmeat basket by Wm. Stephenson, London, 1782, 6in. wide, 9oz.5dwt. $1,125 £500

George III boat-shaped sweetmeat basket by Hester Bateman, London, 1786, 6¾in. long, 6oz. 8dwt. $1,150 £650

George II oval dessert basket by Robt. Brown, London, 1742, 13½in. long, 52oz.1dwt. $3,490 £1,550

One of four George III boat-shaped sweetmeat baskets by Henry Chawner, 1794, 5½in. long, 16oz. 19dwt. $4,725 £2,100

11

Plain tapered cylindrical silver beaker, by John Horsley, London, 1766. $450 £200

George III tapered cylindrical beaker by Thomas Chawner, London, 3in. high, 4oz.8dwt. $745 £330

George III cylindrical beaker by Joseph Creswell, London, 1773, 4in. high, 7oz.2dwt. $745 £330

George II Scottish beaker, 2¾in. high, by Dougal Ged, Edinburgh, 1747, 4oz.17dwt. $835 £370

Late 17th century parcel gilt beaker, 2oz.8dwt., 3¼in. high. $925 £410

Commonwealth plain beaker, London, 1657, 3¾in. high, 7oz. $1,350 £600

Early George III Chester double beaker, 5½in. high, by Richard Richardson, 1767, 6oz.11dwt. $1,465 £650

German parcel gilt cylindrical beaker and cover, Nuremburg, circa 1680, 6oz.2dwt., 6in. high. $1,575 £700

Early 18th century German silver gilt beaker by Esajas Busch, Augsburg, 1705, 3¼in. high, 4oz.12dwt. $1,630 £725

17th century Hungarian parcel gilt beaker, circa 1650, 5¼in. high, 3oz. 17dwt. $1,690 £750

18th century German beaker, 4in. high, circa 1735, 3oz.7dwt.
$1,800 £800

German silver beaker by Paulus Schutte, Hamburg, 1688, 3oz.7dwt.
$1,835 £815

Swedish parcel gilt beaker by Lorentz Lindegren, Boras, 1787, 8½in. high, 12oz.7dwt.$1,980 £880

17th century German silver gilt beaker, 2½in. high, 2oz.18dwt. $2,025 £900

Early 18th century German beaker, 4in. high, Augsburg, circa 1700, 6oz.7dwt.
$2,250 £1,000

German beaker by Godert Bodstede, Hamburg, circa 1660, 4oz.1dwt.
$2,250 £1,000

Swedish parcel gilt beaker on shaped circular domed foot, 13oz.6dwt., 8½in. high, by Johan Adolf Seseman, 1792.
$2,365 £1,050

Swedish parcel gilt beaker by Lorens Stabeus, Stockholm, 1767, 17oz.9dwt., 8¾in. high.$2,365 £1,050

13

17th century Danish tapering cylindrical beaker by Fridrich Kurz, Copenhagen, 1679, 2¾in. high, 2oz. 11dwt. $2,590 £1,150

Swedish parcel gilt beaker by Elias Modin, Sundsvall, circa 1770, 7in. high, 14oz. 5dwt. $2,590 £1,150

Swedish parcel gilt beaker on fluted domed foot, by Didrik Heitmuller, 1777, 16oz.9dwt., 8½in. high. $2,590 £1,150

German parcel gilt beaker and cover, circa 1680, probably by Thomas Ringler, 4oz.3dwt., 4¾in. high. $2,925 £1,300

18th century Swedish parcel gilt beaker, 6in. high, by Friedrich Helinrich Klinck, Stockholm, 1742, 8oz.10dwt. $3,150 £1,400

17th century German parcel gilt beaker by Daniel Manlich, Berlin, 1680, 3oz.14dwt., 3¾in. high. $3,375 £1,500

Swedish parcel gilt beaker by John Wasserman, 1770, 8½in. high, 17oz.17dwt. $3,375 £1,500

Silver gilt beaker by Johann Mittnach, Augsburg, 1736, 6½in. high. $3,600 £1,600

18th century Swedish beaker by Carl Fahlberg, Uppsala, 1777, 12oz.4dwt., 7in. high. $3,600 £1,600

18th century Swedish parcel gilt beaker, by Ekfelt Zacharias, Arboga, 1764, 13oz. 17dwt., 7in. high.
$3,940 £1,750

Early 18th century parcel gilt beaker and cover, 11.8cm. high, 155gm.
$3,940 £1,750

Commonwealth cylindrical silver beaker, London, 1658, 3oz.7dwt., 3¼in. high. $4,390 £1,950

18th century German parcel gilt tapering cylindrical beaker, 5¼in. high, 10oz.
$5,400 £2,400

Dutch beaker on moulded reeded foot, Amsterdam, 1671, 7½in. high, 14oz. 13dwt. $8,550 £3,800

Fine Dutch beaker on corded foot, by Hotze Swerms, Bolsward, 1707, 6¾in. high, 9oz. 17dwt. $11,700 £5,200

Late 17th century Dutch beaker, 7in. high, 12oz.
$16,875 £7,500

Rare silver beaker by I. G. Sneek, 1701.
$18,000 £8,000

Inscribed parcel gilt silver beaker, circa 1560.
$135,000 £60,000

BELLS

18th century Dutch table bell, 4¾in. high, by Jan Bot, Amsterdam, 1748, 8oz.18dwt.
$3,600 £1,600

George I plain table bell by Edmund Holaday, 1716, 6oz.19dwt.
$4,500 £2,000

Good Dutch silver gilt bell by Cornelis de Haan, The Hague, 1775, 5½in. high, 10oz.10dwt.
$5,065 £2,250

BOWLS

 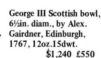 

George II Scottish bowl by Harry Beathune, Edinburgh, 1731, 6in. diam., 7oz.8dwt.
$1,070 £475

George III Scottish bowl, 6½in. diam., by Alex. Gairdner, Edinburgh, 1767, 12oz.15dwt.
$1,240 £550

Early 18th century Italian circular basin, 13½in. diam., 39oz.4dwt. $1,465 £650

18th century silver gilt circular bowl and stand. 63oz.3dwt.
$1,575 £700

George III circular bowl by John Laughlin, Dublin, circa 1750, 18oz., 7in. diam.$2,250 £1,000

George II Irish circular bowl, 6in. diam., by John Hamilton, Dublin, 1737, 13oz.2dwt.
$2,475 £1,100

16

George II provincial bowl by Jonathan Buck, Limerick, circa 1740, 9oz., 5in. diam. $2,475 £1,100

George I Irish bowl, by Philip Kinnersley, Dublin, 1717, 12oz.18dwt., 6½in. diam. $2,590 £1,150

William II small bowl and cover, 4¾in. diam., by Pierre Platel, London, 1700, 12oz.11dwt. $3,040 £1,350

18th century Dutch tub-shaped covered bowl, 3½in. diam., by Marcelis de Haan, The Hague, 6oz. 5dwt. $3,375 £1,500

Early Charles II bleeding bowl, 5½in. diam., London, 1664, 7oz.6dwt. $3,600 £1,600

George II unusual small bowl, 8¼in. diam., by Humphrey Payne, London, 1746, 31oz.2dwt. $4,950 £2,200

George II Scottish bowl, by William Davie, Edinburgh, 12½in. diam. $6,415 £2,850

Small silver bowl, by Thomas Farren, 1717, 8½in. diam., 916gm. $16,875 £7,500

One of a set of four two-handled bowls and stands by S. Herbert & Co., 1751, 110oz. $36,000 £16,000

18th century Dutch brandy bowl, 9¾in. wide, 7oz. 15dwt. **$2,475 £1,100**

18th century oval brandy bowl, 9in. wide, Friesian, 8oz.12dwt.**$2,925 £1,300**

Late 17th century Dutch brandy bowl, by Thos. Sibrand Hicht, Dokkum, 1684, 8½in. wide, 5oz. 14dwt. **$3,715 £1,650**

MONTEITH

Large, late 18th century plated Sheffield Monteith bowl, 12in. high.
$340 £150

William III Monteith bowl, by Robert Peake, London, 1700, 50oz. 10dwt., 11in. diam.
$10,350 £4,600

William III Monteith bowl, by Robert Timbrell, London, 1698, 57oz.4dwt., 11in. diam.
$20,250 £9,000

PUNCH

George III circular punch bowl, 11¼in. diam., by Edward Fernell, London, 1793, 48oz.6dwt.
$2,250 £1,000

Silver punch bowl by William Davie, Edinburgh, 1785, 64oz.
$5,625 £2,500

Rare early American silver punch bowl, by John Coney. **$45,000 £20,000**

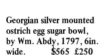

Georgian silver mounted ostrich egg sugar bowl, by Wm. Abdy, 1797, 6in. wide. $565 £250

George III circular sugar bowl, by Matthew West, Dublin, circa 1780, 5½in. diam.. 5oz.10dwt. $610 £270

George II circular sugar bowl, by Richard Williams, Dublin, circa 1752, 5in. diam., 6oz.10dwt. $620 £275

18th century Maltese circular covered sugar bowl, by Gio. Batta Muscat, circa 1790, 5in. high, 6oz. 16dwt. $945 £420

George II covered sugar bowl, 4½in. high, by Francis Crump, London, 1750, 9oz.18dwt. $945 £420

18th century Maltese covered sugar bowl by Francesco Fenech, circa 1780, 5½in. high, 7oz. 16dwt. $1,240 £550

Rare George II Scottish provincial sugar bowl, 4in. diam., by Coline Allan, Aberdeen, circa 1750, 5oz.19dwt. $1,240 £550

George II plain circular sugar bowl and cover, by Matthew E. Lofthouse, 1730, 13oz.9dwt. $3,375 £1,500

Squat silver sugar bowl, by Abraham Pootholt and Jan van Giffen, 1779, 4in. high. $3,600 £1,600

19

Early 18th century circular patch box, ¾in. diam., by Thomas Kedder, London, circa 1705. $305 £135

Small cylindrical box for gaming counters, silver, with slip top, 1680.
$420 £200

William III circular box, 1¾in. diam., by John Cory, London, 1701. $945 £420

Charles II circular box, 2in. diam., London, 1684.
$1,545 £685

Small silver counter box, circa 1650, with pull-off cover. $1,855 £825

Late 18th century Dutch cylindrical biscuit box, 5in. diam., 12oz.19dwt.
$2.250 £1,000

George III Freedom box, by Alex. Ticknell, Dublin, 1797.
$3,265 £1,450

George III Irish silver gilt Freedom box, 3½in. wide, by James Warner, Cork, circa 1787. $3,600 £1,600

17th century Dutch marriage casket, 3in. wide, circa 1630, 3oz.17dwt.
$5,175 £2,300

17th century Dutch silver and enamel spice box, 3.5cm. high. $305 £135

Early 18th century circular covered box, 2¼in. diam. $700 £310

18th century spice box or vinaigrette, probably Danish, 3in. long, 1oz.1dwt. $1,690 £750

Jewish parcel gilt spice box, mid 18th century, 11¼in. high, 9oz.5dwt. $3,825 £1,700

Charles I shell-shaped spice box and spoon, London, 1627, 10oz. 3dwt. $9,000 £4,000

Rare Elizabethan silver spice casket with lion mask handle, by T.B., 23oz. $101,250 £45,000

SUGAR

Early 18th century German shaped oval sugar box and cover, 3¾in. wide, 5oz.1dwt. $1,745 £775

18th century German oval covered sugar box, 4¾in. wide, 6oz.4dwt. $2,700 £1,200

18th century German gilt sugar box of shaped oval form, Augsburg, 1735. $10,125 £4,500

17th century oval silver tobacco box, 4¼in. wide, circa 1680. $1,485 £660

Queen Anne oval tobacco box, by Edward Cornock, London, 1709, 3¾in. wide, 3oz.16dwt. $1,980 £880

William III oval tobacco box, by Nathaniel Locke, 1701, 3oz.12dwt., 3½in. long. $2,815 £1,250

Dutch oblong tobacco box, 1782, 6oz.7dwt., 5½in. long. $4,500 £2,000

18th century Dutch oval tobacco box, 1779, 15oz. 12dwt., 5¾in. high. $4,500 £2,000

Dutch oblong tobacco box, by Evert Bot, Amsterdam, 1755, 6½in. long, 7oz. $7,875 £3,500

Dutch silver tobacco box, Leeuwarden, circa 1750, 22oz.10dwt. $6,750 £3,000

18th century Dutch tobacco box, 6¼in. high, Leiden, 1777, 21oz. 4dwt. $11,475 £5,100

Dutch silver gilt circular tobacco box of bombe form, Middleburg, 1770, 17oz.1dwt. $11,700 £5,200

George III brandy saucepan, 2½in. high, by Robt. Sharp, London, 1798, 6oz.3dwt. $945 £420

George I brandy saucepan, by Erasmus Cope, Dublin, 1717, 1¾in. high, 4oz. $970 £430

George I brandy saucepan, 2¼in. high, by William Fleming, London, 1720, 5oz.17dwt. $1,180 £525

George III silver gilt brandy saucepan, 2¾in. high, by Walter Brind, London, 1763, 5oz.16dwt. $1,180 £525

George III silver saucepan, 4in. high, by F. Knopfell, London, 1768, 19oz.9dwt. $1,565 £695

Plain silver brandy saucepan, by John Le Roux, New York, circa 1740, 14oz.7dwt. $1,620 £720

George II large saucepan, by Wm. Kidney, London, 1737, 4¾in. high, 37oz. 12dwt. $1,735 £770

Early George III brandy saucepan, 4½in. high, by Benjamin Brewood II, London, 1766, 19oz.1dwt. $1,800 £800

Queen Anne brandy saucepan by Daniel Yerbury, London, 1703, 2¼in. high, 4oz.8dwt. $1,800 £800

23

CANDELABRA

One of a pair of George III table candelabra, 16¾in. high, by Henry Hallsworth, London, 1776, 44oz.18dwt.
$2,250 £1,000

One of a pair of George III candelabra, 15¾in. high, by John Winter & Co., Sheffield, 1773.
$2,700 £1,200

One of a pair of 18th century German two-light candelabra, circa 1785, 56oz.2dwt., 14in. high.
$3,150 £1,400

One of a pair of George III two-light candelabra by J. Parker and E. Wakelin, 1774, 14¾in. high, 35oz.
$4,050 £1,800

One of a pair of 18th century German two-light candelabra, 17¼in. high, 72oz.9dwt.
$4,500 £2,000

One of a pair of 18th century German candelabra, Augsburg, 1793-95, 17in. high, 70oz.12dwt.
$6,300 £2,800

One of a pair of George II two-light candelabra, 18in high. $10,800 £4,800

One of a pair of George III silver gilt three-light candelabra, by J. Scofield, London, 1795, 17½in. high, 125oz.
$18,000 £8,000

One of a pair of silver gilt two-light candelabra, by J. Scofield, 1783, 16½in. high. $58,500 £26,000

24

One of a set of four late Victorian, 18th century style, electroplated table candlesticks by Hawksworth, Eyre & Co., 30.8cm. high.
$720 £320

One of a set of four late 18th century silver plated candlesticks, 13in. high.
$830 £370

One of a pair of George III candlesticks, by John Carter, 1769, 12in. high. $870 £385

One of a pair of Belgian table candlesticks, 25cm. high, 1771, 844gm.
$1,305 £580

One of a pair of George III table candlesticks, 11¼in. high, by J. Winter & Co., Sheffield, 1782.
$1,575 £700

One of a pair of George III table candlesticks, by J. Winter & Co., Sheffield, 1780, 11in. high.$1,575 £700

One of a pair of 18th century Austrian table candlesticks, 19oz., 6¾in. high.$1,860 £825

One of a pair of George III table candlesticks, by E. Cooke, London, 1767, 13¾in. high.
$1,980 £880

One of a pair of George II table candlesticks by John Quantock, London, 8in. high, 25oz.8dwt.
$2,025 £900

One of two early George III table candlesticks, by Wm. Cafe, London, 1765, 46oz.11dwt.
$2,250 £1,000

One of four matching George III table candlesticks, 13¾in. high, by John Barbe London, 1765.
$2,475 £1,100

One of a pair of George III table candlesticks, by H. Hobdell, London, 1772, 42oz.10dwt.
$2,590 £1,150

CANDLESTICKS

One of a pair of early George III column candlesticks, by A. Johnston, London, 1760, 14½in. high, 55oz.5dwt.
$2,590 £1,150

One of a pair of early George III table candlesticks, by E. Coker, London, 1763, 10in. high, 37oz.11dwt.
$2,700 · £1,200

One of a pair of George II table candlesticks, by John Preist, London, 1753, 9in. high, 35oz.5dwt.
$2,700 £1,200

One of a pair of 18th century Spanish table candlesticks, circa 1750, 6¾in. high, 17oz.10dwt.
$2,925 £1,300

One of a pair of George II cast silver candlesticks, by J. Cafe, London, 1755, 7¾in. high, 32oz.
$2,925 £1,300

One of a pair of George II table candlesticks, 9¾in. high, by Wm. Cafe, London, 1759.
$2,925 £1,300

One of a pair of George I candlesticks, by James Gould, London, 1725, 16cm. high, 24oz.
$3,375 £1,500

One of a pair of George II table candlesticks, by Thos. England, London, 8in. high, 34oz.2dwt.
$3,375 £1,500

One of a pair of George II caryatid candlesticks, by J. Cafe, London, 1749, 49oz.7dwt., 10in. high.
$3,490 £1,550

One of a pair of 18th century Belgian table candlesticks, Brussels, 1784, 30oz.12dwt., 11½in. high.
$3,490 £1,550

One of a set of four George III table candlesticks, 12¼in. high, by J. Carter, London, 1771.
$3,490 £1,550

One of a set of four George III table candlesticks, by John Lloyd, Dublin, 1772, 10¼in. high, 84oz.
$3,490 £1,550

One of a pair of George II table candlesticks, by T. Parr, London, 1741, 33oz. 17dwt.

$3,600 £1,600

One of a pair of George II cast rococo candlesticks.

$3,715 £1,650

One of a pair of 18th century German table candlesticks, circa 1745, 8½in. high, 21oz. 10dwt.

$3,940 £1,750

One of a pair of George III candlesticks, by J. Carter, London, 1762, 10¼in. high, 37oz. 1dwt.

$4.165 £1,850

One of a pair of George II table candlesticks, by J. Hyatt and C. Semore, London, 1759, 60oz. 8dwt., 11½in. high.

$4,165 £1,850

One of a set of four George III table candlesticks, 12¼in. high, by J. Lambe, London, 1783.

$4,275 £1,900

One of a set of four George III silver table candlesticks, 11in. high, by J. Parsons & Co., Sheffield, 1785.

$4,320 £1,920

One of a set of four George III table candlesticks, by J. Carter, London, 1769, 11¼in. high.

$4,500 £2,000

One of a pair of George II candlesticks, by T. Gilpin, London, 1748, 32oz.8dwt., 8¼in. high.

$4,725 £2,100

One of a pair of James II Irish silver candlesticks with octagonal bases.

$5,175 £2,300

One of a pair of early George II table candlesticks, 6in. high, by J. Luff, London, 1727, 25oz.7dwt.

$5,175 £2,300

One of four matching table candlesticks, by J. Cafe, London, 1751-52, 73oz.11dwt.

$5,290 £2,350

CANDLESTICKS

One of a set of six George III table candlesticks, 12in. high, by J. Green & Co., Sheffield, 1796.
$5,400 £2,400

One of a set of four George II table candlesticks, by J. Cafe, 1750-52, 226oz., 10½in. high.
$5,400 £2,400

One of a pair of George I candlesticks on stepped octagonal bases by R. Bayley, 1724, 17oz.6dwt.
$5,625 £2,500

One of a pair of early George I table candlesticks, by A. Stevenson, London, 1717, 6¼in. high, 14oz. 1dwt.
$5,850 £2,600

One of a pair of Queen Anne cast silver candlesticks, 20½oz., by J. Bird, London, 1713.
$5,965 £2,650

One of four George II Irish table candlesticks, 9½in. high, by Michael Fowler, Dublin, circa 1755, 79oz.12dwt.
$6,190 £2,750

One of four George III table candlesticks, by J. Alleine, 1775, 96oz.
$6,190 £2,750

One of a set of four George II table candlesticks, 9½in. high, by J. Cafe, London, 1750, 108oz.8dwt.
$6,190 £2,750

One of a pair of 18th century Dutch table candlesticks, 12in. high.
$6,975 £3,100

One of a set of four George III candlesticks, by R. Calderwood, Dublin, 1765, 101oz., 14in. high.
$7,875 £3,500

One of four George II table candlesticks, by J. Letablere, Dublin, circa 1740, 8¼in. high, 62oz.
$8,100 £3,600

One of a pair of 18th century Dutch table candlesticks, 6in. high, 14oz. 14dwt.
$9,000 £4,000

One of a pair of
William and Mary
candlesticks, by
F.S.S., London,
1690, 4½in. high,
16oz.8dwt.
$9,450 £4,200

One of a set of
four George III
table candlesticks,
by Wm. Cafe,
1763, 83oz.,
10¾in. high.
$9,900 £4,400

One of a set of
four silver table
candlesticks, by
G. Wickes, London,
1739, 65oz.
$12,375 £5,500

One of a set of four
small table candle-
sticks, by Wm.
Gould, 1732, 44oz.
$14,400 £6,400

One of a pair of
17th century sil-
ver candlesticks,
7½in. high.
$17,550 £7,800

One of a set of four
Queen Anne table
candlesticks.
$20,815 £9,250

One of a set of four
silver table candle-
sticks, by Simon le
Sage, London, 1759,
28.5cm. high, 141oz.
2dwt.
$24,750 £11,000

One of a set of six
table candlesticks,
by N. Clausen, 1718,
21.6cm. high.
$45,000 £20,000

One of four George
II table candlesticks,
by Paul de Lamerie,
6½in. high, London,
1731, 65oz.15dwt.
$47,250 £21,000

One of a pair of
Dutch silver table
candlesticks, Delft,
1677, 8½in. high,
29oz.
$48,310 £21,740

One of a pair of
Louis XVI silver
candlesticks, by J.
Besnier, Paris,
27cm. high.
$49,500 £22,000

One of a pair of 17th
century silver candle-
sticks, by J. Bodendick,
9¼in. high.
$90,000 £40,000

29

CASTERS

A small vase-shaped George III silver sugar caster, circa 1793. $165 £75

George II sugar caster with pierced lid, by T. Wynne, 1759, 19.5cm. high, 7¾oz. $655 £290

George II vase-shaped caster, 6in. high, London, 1740, 5oz.11dwt. $675 £300

George II Scottish baluster caster, 6in. high, 5oz.16dwt. $755 £335

A set of three George III silver casters, by Wm. Davie, Edinburgh, 1770, 14oz. $1,135 £505

Early 18th century octagonal caster by Charles Adam, London, 8¼in. high, 12oz.14dwt. $1,235 £550

George III baluster caster by James Warner, Cork, circa 1790, 5¾in. high, 3oz. $1,350 £600

Queen Anne cylindrical caster with pierced lid, 6½in. high, 6oz.17dwt. $1,350 £600

George I vase-shaped caster, Dublin, 1717, 9oz. 7¼in. high. $1,440 £640

George II vase-shaped caster, by Thomas Bamford, London, 1729, 6in. high, 5oz.15dwt. **$1,575 £700**

George I octagonal caster, by Glover Johnson, London, 1717, 6oz.13dwt. **$1,600 £715**

Early 18th century German caster, circa 1720, 6½in. high, 5oz.3dwt. **$1,675 £745**

George I vase-shaped caster, 8¼in. high, by Louis Cuny, London, 1722, 14oz.9dwt. **$1,800 £800**

Set of three George III casters, by John Delmester, London, 1762, 18oz.8dwt. **$1,855 £825**

George I plain octagonal pear-shaped caster, by Thos. Bamford, 1719, 7½in. high, 9oz.11dwt. **$2,250 £1,000**

Queen Anne caster, London, 1713, by Charles Adams, 6½in. high, 7oz. **$2,700 £1,200**

Rare 18th century cape caster, 6in. high, by Gerhardus Lotter, circa 1790, 6oz.13dwt. **$2,700 £1,200**

George I vase-shaped caster, 8½in. high, by Samuel Margas, 1716, 16oz.2dwt. **$3,150 £1,400**

CASTERS

Set of three George I octagonal casters, by John Pero, London, 1717, 17oz. 3dwt., 6¼in. and 5in. high.
$3,375 £1,500

18th century Flemish vase-shaped caster, 7½in. high, Malines, circa 1710, 8oz.19dwt.
$3,940 £1,750

Set of three George II baluster casters, 8¾in. and 7¼in. high, by Samuel Wood, London, 1751, 41oz.9dwt.
$4,165 £1,850

18th century Flemish vase-shaped caster, 7½in. high, circa 1710, 8oz.19dwt.
$4,275 £1,900

A set of three George I plain vase-shaped casters, by Paul Crespin, 1723, 33oz. $4,500 £2,000

George II octagonal caster, by Gabriel Sleath, London, 1727, 6¾in. high, 9oz. 9dwt. $4,500 £2,000

George I large plain caster, by John Sanders, 1719, 23.5cm. high.
$5,065 £2,250

Dutch vase-shaped fluted caster, by Reynier de Haan, 1756, 16oz.4dwt.
$6,750 £3,000

Charles II silver caster, the cover pierced with trefoils and quatrefoils, circa 1672, 7in. high. $22,500 £10,000

Unusual table centrepiece, 17in. long, circa 1770, 45oz.   **$1,350 £600**

George III silver gilt 'Gazebo' centrepiece, 21¼in. high, by Wm. Pitts and J. Preedy, London, 1791, 111oz.4dwt.   **$5,625 £2,500**

The Macready Testimonial, a large silver centrepiece. **$27,000 £12,000**

CHALICES

18th century Italian chalice and paten, by Giovanni Valadier, Rome, 10¼in. high, circa 1775, 24oz.10dwt.   **$1,395 £620**

Rare Elizabeth I chalice, 6in. high, circa 1580, 6oz.14dwt.   **$1,690 £750**

Elizabeth I provincial chalice, by E. Coke, circa 1580, 6in. high, 6oz.14dwt.   **$2,250 £1,000**

Elizabeth I chalice and cover, 1570, 7in. high, 8oz. 16dwt.   **$5,175 £2,300**

Rare Elizabethan provincial chalice, 5¾in. high, Norwich, 1567, 6oz.18dwt.   **$7,200 £3,200**

Rare German gilt metal chalice, by Marcus Purman, 1608, 12.4cm. high.   **$58,500 £26,000**

CHAMBERSTICKS

George III silver chamber-
stick, by Hester Bateman,
London, 1787, 6in. diam.
$385 £170

George II chamber candle-
stick, by Elizabeth God-
frey, London, 1750, 6in.
high, 14oz. $655 £290

George III chamber candle-
stick, 5¼in. diam., by J.
Lambe, London, 1785.
$755 £335

George III silver chamber-
stick, by John Scofield,
13½oz., London, 1778.
$790 £350

George I chamber can-
dlestick, by Sarah
Holaday, London, 1721,
4½in. diam., 10oz.
$790 £350

George III chamber candle-
stick, by Wm. Lancester,
London, 1774, 8oz.18dwt.,
5¾in. diam. $1,125 £500

George IIII chamber can-
dlestick, 6in. diam., by
Ebenezer Coker, London,
1768, 9oz.16dwt.
$1,195 £530

One of a pair of George III
Scottish chamber candle-
sticks, 5½in. diam., by P.
Robertson, Edinburgh,
1786, 25oz.1dwt.
$2,250 £1,000

One of a pair of George II
chamber candlesticks, by
Phillips Garden, London,
1742, 5¾in. diam., 24oz.
12dwt. $2,475 £1,100

James II chamber candle-
stick, 3½in. diam., 2oz.,
maker's mark T.E.
$2,645 £1,175

George II chamber candle-
stick, by P. Crespin, London, 1744, 7in. wide, 11oz.
17dwt. $4,165 £1,850

One of a pair of King
Adolphus of Sweden silver
candlesticks, by Mattias
Grahl, Goteburg, 1752.
$9,000 £4,000

34

18th century German silver gilt chocolate pot, 9¼in. high. **$1,920 £850**

Queen Anne plain tapering cylindrical chocolate pot, 9¼in. high, by A. Nelme, 1704, 18oz.16dwt. **$2,700 £1,200**

Louis XV baluster chocolate pot, 6½in. high, Paris, 1773. **$2,815 £1,250**

French plain pear-shaped chocolate pot, by Alex. de Roussy, Paris, 1779, 6¼in. high, 9oz.2dwt. **$2,925 £1,300**

George III baluster chocolate pot, London, 11in. high, 30oz.6dwt. **$3,715 £1,650**

18th century German chocolate pot, 7¼in. high, by Johann Heinrich Menzel, Augsburg, circa 1735, 15oz.1dwt. **$4,500 £2,000**

Large pear-shaped chocolate pot, 26cm. high, circa 1740. **$4,950 £2,200**

Louis XIV baluster chocolate pot, 8in. high, Paris, 1692. **$6,075 £2,700**

Large Louis XV chocolate pot, by Toussaint Bingant, Paris, 1750. **$6,075 £2,700**

CHOCOLATE POTS

Rare George III baluster chocolate pot, by R. Williams, Dublin, circa 1770, 10in. high, 36oz.
$6,415 £2,850

Queen Anne tapered cylindrical chocolate pot, by R. Timbrell and J. Bell, London, 1711, 25oz.11dwt., 10in. high. $8,550 £3,800

George II tapered cylindrical chocolate pot, by Isaac Cookson, Newcastle, 1732.
$9,000 £4,000

Silver chocolate pot, by T. Bolton, Dublin, 1706, 25.4cm. high, 25oz.8dwt.
$9,000 £4,000

Short spouted chocolate pot, by David Willaume, Jnr., 1744, 10¼in. high, 45oz.10dwt., with wickerwork handle.
$9,565 £4,250

Queen Anne plain tapering cylindrical chocolate pot, by Joseph Ward, 1706, 27oz., 10½in. high.
$11,700 £5,200

Fine cylindrical silver chocolate pot, 1725, 9in. high, 26oz.10dwt., made by Joseph Clare.
$16,875 £7,500

An Irish chocolate pot, dated 1721.
$16,875 £7,500

Queen Anne tapered cylindrical chocolate pot, by Wm. Fawdrey, London, 1706, 25oz.18dwt.
$18,565 £8,250

Pierced Sheffield plate wine coaster with wooden base, circa 1790. $170 £75

One of a pair of George III circular coasters, by Daniel Pontifex, London, 1799, 6¼in. diam. $1,000 £450

One of a pair of George III wine coasters, 5in. diam., by Philip Freeman, London, 1773. $1,180 £525

One of a set of four George III silver wine coasters, by Wm. Plummer, 1777. $1,350 £600

Two of a set of four George III circular wine coasters, 4¼in. diam., by Wm. Abdy I, London, 1788. $1,575 £700

One of a set of three George III silver coasters, by R. Hennell, London, 1780. $1,575 £700

One of a pair of George III wine coasters, by R. Hennell, London, 1793, 4½in. diam. $1,800 £800

One of a set of four circular wine coasters, by Thos. Jackson II, London, 1774, 4¾in. diam. $2,025 £900

One of a set of four George III circular pierced coasters, by R. Hennell, 12.5cm. diam. $2,475 £1,100

A pair of George III silver gilt wine coasters on a gilt metal four-wheeled wagon, 5in. diam., by M. Plummer, London, 1792. $2,815 £1,250

One of a pair of George III decanter wagons, 12¾in. wide, by Nathaniel Smith & Co., Sheffield, 1799. $5,625 £2,500

One of a set of four George III silver gilt wine coasters, 5½in. diam., by D. Scott and B. Smith. $12,375 £5,500

37

COFFEE POTS

Sheffield plate baluster coffee pot, circa 1760.
$475 £210

Plain pear-shaped plated coffee pot on circular foot, circa 1760, 13in. high.
$810 £360

Russian vase-shaped small coffee pot, 8in. high, Moscow, circa 1790, 10oz. 2dwt.
$900 £400

George II coffee pot by John Pero, 15oz., 18.5cm. high.
$1,350 £600

George III coffee pot, by Robert Swanson, London, 1765.
$1,600 £710

George II tapered cylindrical coffee pot, by Gabriel Sleath, circa 1745, 9in. high, 22oz.5dwt.
$1,610 £715

Early George III baluster coffee pot, 11¾in. high, by Wm. Grundy, London, 1763, 31oz. $1,675 £745

George II silver coffee pot, by Richard Beale, London, 1731, 15½oz., 20.5cm. high.
$1,745 £775

George III baluster coffee pot, by Benjamin Gignac, London, 1767, 11¼in. high, 31oz.15dwt.
$1,800 £800

George III baluster coffee pot, by J. Robins, London, 1788, 23oz.9dwt., 11½in. high. $1,860 £825

George II tapering cylindrical coffee pot, by T. Farren, London, 1738, 22oz.3dwt., 9¼in. high. $1,860 £825

George III coffee pot, 10¾in. high, by T. Whipham and C. Wright, London, 1763, 34oz.9dwt. $1,890 £840

George II tapering cylindrical coffee pot, 9½in. high, by H. Brind, London, 1749, 24oz.12dwt. $1,890 £840

George III coffee pot, sold with a teapot and milk jug, 11¾in. high, by Urquhart and Hart, London, 1799, 42oz.16dwt. $2,080 £925

George II coffee pot, 10¼in. high, by William Cripps, 1745, 32oz. $2,140 £950

George II tapering cylindrical coffee pot, London, 1742, by J. Fossy, 24oz. $2,140 £950

George I tapered cylindrical coffee pot, by P. Archambo, London, 1724, 9½in. high, 27oz.12dwt. $2,140 £950

George II tapering cylindrical coffee pot, 8¾in. high, by Thomas Farren, London, 1741, 22oz.2dwt. $2,140 £950

COFFEE POTS

George II tapering cylindrical coffee pot, by John le Sage, London, circa 1735, 9¾in. high.
$2,250 £1,000

George III coffee pot, by R. & D. Hennell, 1795, 12¾in. high, 25oz.4dwt.
$2,250 £1,000

George III silver coffee pot, by Wm. Bayley, London, 1784, 12in. high.
$2,250 £1,000

George II coffee pot, by T. Rush, London, 1744, 10¼in. high, 28oz.
$2,250 £1,000

George II baluster coffee pot, by Shaw & Priest, London, 1757, 9¾in. high, 26oz.4dwt.
$2,250 £1,000

George II tapering cylindrical coffee pot, by Charles Sprage, London, 1736, 9½in. high, 26oz.19dwt.
$2,250 £1,000

George III baluster coffee pot, by C. Wright, London, 1772, 11½in. high, 29oz. 16dwt. $2,250 £1,000

George III baluster coffee pot, by D. Smith and R. Sharp, London, 1768, 20oz.16dwt., 11¾in. high.
$2,250 £1,000

George II baluster coffee pot, by Fuller White, London, 1758, 10½in. high, 27oz.8dwt.
$2,475 £1,100

George III coffee pot, by
H. Chawner, London,
1786, 23oz.
$2,590 £1,150

George II tapering cylin-
drical coffee pot, by R.
Gurney & Co., London,
8¾in. high, 27oz.1dwt.
$2,700 £1,200

18th century German coffee
pot, 11¼in. high, by Johann
Christian Neuss, Augsburg,
1799, 23oz.6dwt.
$2,700 £1,200

George II tapering cylindrical coffee pot, by John Hugh
le Sage, London, 1743, 27oz.
2dwt., 9½in. high.
$2,815 £1,250

George II tapered coffee
pot, 9½in. high, by T.
Whipham and Wm.
Williams, London, 1742,
27oz.6dwt.
$2,815 £1,250

George III baluster coffee
pot, by R. Morton & Co.,
Sheffield, 1778, 11½in.
high, 23oz.10dwt.
$2,815 £1,250

George II cylindrical coffee
pot, 7½in. high, by A.
Buteux, 1729, 18oz.14dwt.
$2,815 £1,250

Coffee pot by Thomas
Wirgman, London, 1751,
26oz. $2,815 £1,250

George II coffee pot, by I.
Cookson, Newcastle, 1750,
9in. high, 26oz.
$2,925 £1,300

41

COFFEE POTS

18th century Swiss coffee pot, 7¾in. high, maker's mark L.B.D., circa 1760, 11oz.18dwt.
$2,925 £1,300

George II tapered cylindrical pot, 8½in. high, by G. Sleath, London, 1739, 20oz.16dwt.
$2,925 £1,300

Italian fluted pear-shaped coffee pot, 10½in. high, circa 1775, 24oz.
$3,150 £1,400

George II tapering coffee pot, 8¾in. high, by John Swift, London, 1739, 26oz.18dwt.
$3,375 £1,500

George III silver coffee pot, by Young and Jackson, London, 1774, 11¼in. high.
$3,375 £1,500

Individual coffee pot, 5½in. high, 8oz., 1727, by Peze Pilleau. $3,375 £1,500

Silver coffee pot, by James Schruder, 1741, with scrolling work on base, 8¾in. high, 25oz.3dwt.
$3,375 £1,500

George I tapering coffee pot, by Richard Bayley, 1720, 10¼in. high, 28oz.
$3,490 £1,550

George III plain pear-shaped coffee pot, by David Whyte, 1769, 11in. high, 32oz. $3,600 £1,600

George II silver coffee pot, by R. Calderwood, Dublin, circa 1760. $3,600 £1,600

George I plain tapering coffee pot, by Isaac Liger, 1725, 15oz., 7¼in. high. $3,600 £1,600

Vase-shaped silver coffee pot, by Daniel Smith and Robert Sharp, 1776, 11in. high, 24oz. $3,940 £1,750

18th century Swiss coffee pot, 8¼in. high, Geneva, circa 1770, 16oz. $3,940 £1,750

George II plain cylindrical coffee pot, by Edward Feline, 1728, 9½in. high, 26oz. $4,500 £2,000

George III baluster coffee pot, by Wm. Grundy, London, 1770, 10¾in. high, 31oz.2dwt. $4,950 £2,200

George II tapered cylindrical coffee pot, by John Barbe, London, 1746, 6¼in. high, 12oz.3dwt. $5,175 £2,300

Early George II tapered cylindrical coffee pot by Peze Pilleau, London, 1733, 8in. high, 22oz. 1dwt. $5,175 £2,300

George III baluster coffee pot, by Hester Bateman, London, 1787, 24oz.5dwt., 12¼in. high. $5,400 £2,400

COFFEE POTS

George II baluster coffee pot, by Fuller White, London, 1754, 11¼in. high, 41oz. 3dwt. $5,625 £2,500

18th century German coffee pot, 11¼in. high, by Diedrich Bockstover, Quakenbruck, circa 1755, 25oz.18dwt.
$6,415 £2,850

George II tapering cylindrical coffee pot, 13in. high, by John Swift, London, 1751, 55oz.19dwt.
$7,200 £3,200

Side-handled coffee pot, by David Tanqueray, 9½in. high, 33oz.10dwt.
$9,450 £4,250

George I cylindrical coffee pot, by Paul de Lamerie, 1723, 27oz.$9,450 £4,250

George I silver coffee pot, by Thomas Farrer, London, 1722.
$10,125 £4,500

Rare Channel Islands silver coffee pot, 34oz., 1740.
$13,500 £6,000

George II fine plain tapering cylindrical coffee pot, by Paul de Lamerie, 1730, 7¾in. high; 23oz.
$28,125 £12,500

A magnificent George II silver coffee pot, by de Lamerie, made in 1738.
$78,750 £35,000

George III silver creamboat, by Wm. Harrison, 1763. $450 £200

George II creamboat, 5¼in., by William Cripps, London, 1743, 6oz.2dwt. $1,240 £550

George II Scottish cream-boat, by John Main, Edin-burgh, 1739, 6½in. wide, 7oz.14dwt.$1,735 £770

CRUETS

Dutch silver cruet frame of waisted oblong form, Amsterdam, 1772, 16oz. 19dwt. $1,015 £450

George III oval cruet frame and bottles, by Robert and David Hennell, London, 1799. $1,350 £600

George II cinquefoil cruet, 9½in. high, by Samuel Wood, London, 1744, 45oz.1dwt. $1,860 £825

George III cruet frame, by Paul Storr, 11½in. high, 31oz.1dwt., with six cut glass bottles. $2,250 £1,000

George III cruet frame by Paul Storr, 12½in. wide, 36oz.2dwt. $2,815 £1,250

Pair of 17th century Spanish silver gilt altar cruets and a tazza, 4½in. high and 9¾in. diam., 47oz.2dwt. $3,600 £1,600

45

George II cinquefoil cruet frame, by S. Wood, London, 1737, 9¼in. high, 59oz.
$3,825 £1,700

One of a pair of Louis XVI two-bottle cruets, 12¾in. wide, by Jacques Favre, Paris, 1778, 51oz.1dwt.
$3,825 £1,700

18th century German two-bottle cruet frame, 9½in. high, by Elias Adam, Augsburg, circa 1735, 8oz.13dwt.
$4,275 £1,900

George III cruet frame, by Paul Storr, 14¾in. wide.
$4,725 £2,100

George II cruet frame with castors and bottles, by Jabez Daniell, 1749, 55oz. $5,625 £2,500

George II two-bottle cruet frame, by George Wickes, London, 1742, 12oz., 8¾in. high. $5,850 £2,600

Early George II two-bottle cruet frame, by Paul de Lamerie, London, 1728, 5½in. wide, 14oz.13dwt.
$11,250 £5,000

Double oval shaped cruet stand, by Frantz Peter Bunsen, Hanover, circa 1794, 2,120gm., 32.5cm. long.
$19,225 £8,545

George II cinquefoil cruet, by Paul de Lamerie, 1733, 60oz.18dwt.
$19,350 £8,600

Queen Anne Britannia silver two-handled cup, London, 1706, 4oz., 2¾in. high. $450 £200

18th century Channel Islands christening cup, 2¾in. high. $640 £285

Silver loving cup, by Hester Bateman, circa 1789. $820 £365

George III vase-shaped cup and cover, 13¼in. high, by James Young, London, 1784, 53oz.18dwt. $1,015 £450

George I Britannia silver cup and cover, by Wm. Gamble, London, 1717, 29½oz., 24.5cm. high. $1,240 £550

George III silver gilt two-handled cup and cover, 13¾in. high, by F. Butty and N. Dumee, 1766, 51oz. $1,240 £550

George II two-handled cup, by Lothian & Robertson, Edinburgh, 1755, 48oz. 5dwt., 8in. high. $1,465 £650

George III Irish cup and cover, by Joseph Jackson, Dublin, 1784, 17½in. high, 68oz.2dwt. $1,465 £650

Coconut cup with 17th century silver mounts, bearing an inscription, 3½in. diam. $1,485 £660

CUPS

George II silver gilt two-handled cup and cover, by John Le Sage, London, 1736, 24oz.1dwt., 8¼in. high. $1,635 £725

One of a pair of George II Irish two-handled cups, 4¾in. high, by Robert Calderwood, Dublin, circa 1740, 27oz.6dwt.
$1,680 £745

George III two-handled cup and cover, by Francis Crump, 1762, 32oz.
$1,690 £750

George I silver gilt cup and cover, 12in. high, by Ed. Vincent, London, 1723, 78oz.1dwt. $1,800 £800

George III two-handled cup and cover, 18½in. high, by John Robins, London, 1786, 117oz. 3dwt. $1,980 £880

Queen Anne two-handled cup and cover, 10½in. high, by David Willaume, London, 1712, 54oz.16dwt.
$2,475 £1,100

Two-handled silver mounted serpentine cup and cover, circa 1675, 7¼in. high.
$2,700 £1,200

Silver cup and cover, Irish, Dublin, 1748, 37.5cm. high, 150oz.
$4,500 £2,000

Late 16th century parcel gilt pineapple cup, by Martin Dumling, Nuremburg.
$4,725 £2,100

Early 18th century German wager cup, 16.8cm. high, 190gm. $5,400 £2,400

Early 17th century silver gilt standing cup, 11¼in. high, by A. Tittecke, Nuremburg, circa 1600, 11oz.11dwt.
$6,300 £2,800

George III silver gilt two-handled cup and cover, by Smith & Sharp, London, 1772, 17¾in. high, 121oz. 2dwt. $8,550 £3,800

Coconut cup and cover, circa 1632, with mid 18th century additions, 9½in. high. $9,450 £4,200

Early 17th century cup and cover, by Johan Janes, Hamburg. $11,475 £5,100

Rare 17th century German parcel gilt horn-shaped cup, 13cm. high, 375gm.
$19,125 £8,500

Commonwealth two-handled cup and cover, marked on base and lid, maker's mark A. F. in a shaped shield, London, 1653. $45,000 £20,000

One of a set of four silver communion cups, by Patrick Borthwick, Edinburgh, 1645.
$135,000 £60,000

An exceptionally fine T'ang dynasty silver gilt stem cup.
$146,250 £65,000

Charles II caudle cup, 2½in. high, London, 1664, 2oz.9dwt.
$1,575 £700

Charles II caudle cup and cover, by Garthorne, London, 1682, 22oz.6dwt., 6½in. high.$9,000 £4,000

Commonwealth silver gilt caudle cup and cover, by N. Wollaston, London, 1656, 4½in. high, 13oz.12dwt.
$10,800 £4,800

STIRRUP

Late 18th century silver fox mask stirrup cup.$270 £120

Late 18th century fox mask stirrup cup.
$360 £160

George III stirrup cup, 5½in. long, by Thomas Pitts, London, 1770, 6oz. 2dwt. $2,250 £1,000

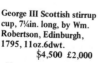

George III Scottish stirrup cup, 7¼in. long, by Wm. Robertson, Edinburgh, 1795, 11oz.6dwt.
$4,500 £2,000

A pair of silver gilt fox mask stirrup cups, Sheffield, 1786, 4¾in. long.
$4,950 £2,200

One of a pair of George III parcel gilt stirrup cups, by John Carter, London, 1773.
$7,315 £3,250

50

18th century Norwegian parcel gilt tumbler cup, 1oz.9dwt., 1¾in. high. $900 £400

Queen Anne provincial tumbler cup, by John Langwith, York, 1708, 1¾in. high, 1oz.18dwt. $1,440 £640

One of a set of three early 18th century parcel gilt tumbler cups, circa 1700, 9oz.2dwt.$2,250 £1,000

WINE

George III wine cup, by Walter Brind, London, 1781, 5½in. high, 12oz. 19dwt. $675 £300

George III wine cup, 6in. high, by Hester Bateman, London, 1787, 5oz. 19dwt. $900 £400

Elizabeth I small communion cup on domed spreading foot, provincial, unidentified mark, circa 1570, 4oz.12dwt. $1,800 £800

Unusual Charles II wine cup, circa 1675, 3½in. high, 2oz.6dwt. $2,700 £1,200

German silver gilt owl drinking cup, 7in. high, late 16th century. $7,200 £3,200

James I silver gilt wine cup, 8in. high, London, 1610, 10oz.12dwt.$7,200 £3,200

Silver chafing dish with Belgian hall marks, 1772. $655 £290

18th century South American shaving dish, 17½in. wide, circa 1760, 38oz. 5dwt. $700 £310

One of a pair of 18th century silver scallop shell butter dishes, Dublin, 9¾oz. $720 £320

18th century oval dessert dish, 11¼in. wide, circa 1765, 21oz.8dwt. $810 £360

A circular silver Queen Anne footed waiter. $1,080 £480

18th century East European parcel gilt dish and cover, 10¾in. diam. 22oz.5dwt. $1,125 £500

Large South American sideboard dish, 16¾in. diam., 18th century, 62oz.12dwt. $1,215 £540

17th century German silver gilt circular dish, 10½in. diam., 7oz.5dwt. $1,735 £770

George III altar dish, 21¼in. diam., by Robert Gaze, London, 1796. $2,025 £900

One of a pair of George I silver gilt strawberry dishes, 8½in. diam., London, 1719, 24oz.18dwt.
$2,250 £1,000

One of two late 18th century oval butter dishes, 7½in. wide, 17oz.9dwt.
$2,475 £1,100

Charles II plain circular alms dish, 10¼in. diam., 18oz.14dwt.
$2,475 £1,100

William III plain credence paten, 3¾in. high, 7oz. 16dwt. $2,835 £1,260

George III oblong toasted cheese dish, by Paul Storr, London, 1797, 9¼in. wide, 34oz.11dwt.
$3,715 £1,650

Louis XV plain circular ecuelle and cover with shell-shaped handles, maker's mark F.B.D., Arras, circa 1750, 17oz. 11dwt. $10,125 £4,500

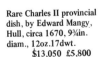

Rare Charles II provincial dish, by Edward Mangy, Hull, circa 1670, 9¼in. diam., 12oz.17dwt.
$13,050 £5,800

17th century Dutch silver embossed dish, maker's mark H.N., Hague, 1666, 82oz. $101,250 £45,000

A T'ang dynasty silver engraved and gilt dish, 30.5cm. diam.
$112,500 £50,000

George III entree dish and cover, 12¼in. wide, by J. Edwards, London, 41oz. 14dwt. $1,240 £550

George III oval entree dish and cover, by T. Daniel, London, 1787, 49oz.18dwt.
$1,610 £715

George III bacon dish, by Michael Plummer, London, 1791, 14oz., 11in. wide.
$1,935 £860

One of a pair of entree dishes, by Wm. Frisbee, London, 1799, 96oz.1dwt.
$1,970 £875

One of a pair of George III entree dishes and covers, 10¼in. wide, by J. Scofield, London, 1798, 79oz.10dwt.
$4,050 £1,800

One of a pair of George III entree dishes and covers, by Paul Storr, 12in. long, 135oz. $13,500 £6,000

MEAT

One of three George III oval meat dishes, 12in. wide, by Wm. Cripps, London, 1760, 61oz.3dwt.
$2,250 £1,000

One of a pair of George II oval meat dishes, by Simon Jouet, 1759, 18in. long, 124oz.
$4,500 £2,000

One of a pair of Louis XV oval shaped meat dishes, by Alexis Loir, Paris, 1744, 103oz.
$49,500 £22,000

54

17th century German sweetmeat dish, Augsburg, circa
1675, 5¼in. wide, 2oz.9dwt.
$1,395 £620

German oval sweetmeat
dish, circa 1685, 2oz.
10dwt., 5in. wide.
$1,540 £685

Charles I two-handled oval
sweetmeat dish, 6¾in.
long, 2oz.15dwt.
$2,250 £1,000

Charles I circular shaped
sweetmeat dish, 6¾in. diam.,
London, 1638, 4oz.16dwt.
$3,150 £1,400

Charles I shaped circular
sweetmeat dish, 6¾in.
diam., London, 1631,
4oz.16dwt.
$3,150 £1,400

A very fine silver sweetmeat
box, maker's mark B.B. with
a crescent below, London,
1676, 18.4cm., 21oz.12dwt.
$56,250 £25,000

VEGETABLE

One of a pair of George III
circular vegetable dishes
and covers, 9¼in. diam.,
by Wakelin & Garrard,
London, 1796, 64oz.12dwt.
$2,475 £1,100

One of a pair of George
III plain circular vegetable
dishes and covers, 10½in.
diam., by Paul Storr,
1808, 116oz.
$3,825 £1,700

George III circular vegetable
dish and cover, by Paul
Storr, London, 1796, 107oz.
1dwt., 12¾in. diam.
$3,940 £1,750

EPERGNES

George III epergne, by Emick Romer, London, 1770, 91oz. 19dwt., 17¼in. high.
$2,250 £1,000

George III silver epergne with pierced baskets.
$2,815 £1,250

George III table centrepiece, by Thomas Powell, London, 1768, 77oz. $4,840 £2,150

George III epergne, by Thos. Pitts, London, 1788, 16in. high, 124oz. $5,965 £2,650

George III epergne, 17in. high, by Thos. Pitts, London, 1789, 121oz.
$6,750 £3,000

George III epergne, 15¼in. high, by Thos. Pitts, London, 1774, 129oz.12dwt.
$7,875 £3,500

George III epergne, by Robert Hennell, 1781, 16¾in. high, 147oz. $8,665 £3,850

George III epergne, by Thos. Pitts, 1778, 152oz., 17in. high.
$11,700 £5,200

George II silver gilt epergne, by Wm. Cripps, London, 1751, 12in. high, 172oz.8dwt.
$13,050 £5,800

18th century Spanish
baluster covered ewer, 11in.   17th century Italian   Spanish parcel gilt ewer,
high, probably Cadiz, 1787,   ewer, Naples, 24oz.10dwt., 11in. high, mid 16th century,
23oz.10dwt. $3,600 £1,600   9in. high. $4,500 £2,000   34oz.16dwt.$19,125 £8,500

17th century helmet-
shaped ewer, 7¼in. high,
21oz.4dwt.   Silver ewer and basin by   Early 17th century
        $27,000 £12,000   Christian van Vianen, Utrecht, Dutch silver gilt ewer.
                               1632. $337,500 £150,000 $45,000 £20,000

FISH SLICES

Silver fish trowel by Richard Williams,   18th century Dutch fish slice, 4oz.
1770, 13in. long. $900 £400   14dwt. $1,485 £660

18th century Dutch serving slice,   18th century Dutch fish slice, by
15¼in. long, by Wm. Pont, Amsterdam,   Jan Diederik Pont, 1760, 15in.
1772, 6oz.14dwt. $1,685 £750   long, 6oz.15dwt. $2,590 £1,150

FLATWARE

A matching silver fork and spoon, 1760. $75 £30

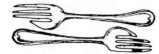

Pair of 18th century oyster forks, Old English thread. $135 £60

18th century South Italian boxwood handled knife, 33.5cm. long. $550 £245

Set of miniature George II Hanoverian spoons, a mote skimmer and another spoon, with pair of sugar nips, circa 1730. $1,215 £540

Rare early 17th century French two-prong fork. $1,870 £830

58

Early butter knife, by Thomas Wallis, London, 1798. $80 £35

Travelling knife and fork set, knife with double duty mark, in case, circa 1798. $170 £75

17th century silver sucket fork with rat tail bowl, by T.A., London, 1690. $700 £310

Rare 18th century travelling companion which is also a knife and fork set. $1,125 £500

Dutch travelling knife, fork and spoon set, circa 1700. $1,485 £660

One of a set of twelve pairs of silver gilt and amber dessert knives and forks, mid 18th century. $1,980 £880

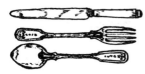

Part of a George III silver gilt dessert service, London, 1799. $2,590 £1,150

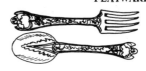

Louis XIV trefid spoon and four-prong fork, Paris, 1675. $2,700 £1,200

One of two Louis XIV three-prong forks, by Matthurin Villian, Paris, 1677. $3,150 £1,400

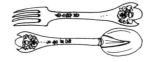

Rare, Louis XIV trefid spoon and four-prong fork. $4,335 £1,925

Part of a composite Old English pattern table service, circa 1776-1782. $8,550 £3,800

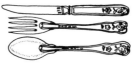

Part of a set of twelve Louis XV silver gilt dessert knives, forks and spoons. $10,125 £4,500

Part of a Queen Anne table service of thirty-six pieces. $10,125 £4,500

Louis XIV silver gilt spoon and fork, by Marin Marie, Paris, 1681. $10,125 £4,500

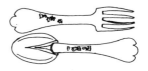

Two of six pieces of Louis XIV table silver by Louis Nicolle, circa 1687. $24,750 £11,000

FLATWARE
SPOONS

Jersey feather edge tablespoon, by J. Quesney, circa 1800. $100 £45

Tablespoon by Hester Bateman, London, 1766. $160 £70

One of six Scandinavian silver tablespoons, 18th century, 11oz. $290 £130

Late Roman/Byzantine silver spoon, 4th-5th century A.D. $415 £185

18th century Danish spoon, by Jens Christensen, Copenhagen. $430 £190

14th century Paris made spoon with circular bowl. $510 £225

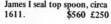

James I seal top spoon, circa 1611. $560 £250

17th century seal top spoon of East Anglican origin. $585 £260

One of a pair of William III trefid spoons, London 1696, maker probably John Spackman, 3oz.15dwt. $820 £275

17th century Scandinavian spoon, probably Danish. $820 £275

17th century Scandinavian spoon, with engraved stem. $640 £285

Charles I seal top spoon, London, 1639. $655 £290

Mid 16th century Moor's head spoon. $670 £310

17th century Norwegian parcel gilt spoon, by Jorgen Bleckman.$720 £320

17th century Norwegian spoon, by Oluf Jorgensen, Bergen. $720 £320

Early 18th century Norwegian spoon, by Johannes Johannesen Reimers of Bergen, circa 1705. $790 £350

West Country 'Buddha Knop' spoon, circa 1640. $770 £355

One of six scroll top dessert spoons, by Hester Bateman, 1784, 5oz. $810 £360

Charles I slip top spoon, London, 1640. $900 £400

Early 17th century apostle spoon, Carlisle, circa 1600. $900 £400

Early 17th century seal top spoon, circa 1620, possibly Beccles. $900 £400

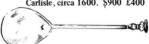

Plain James I seal top spoon, London, 1606, 6½in. long. $1,125 £500

17th century provincial apostle spoon, by Wm. Ramsay, Newcastle, circa 1660. $1,170 £520

James I apostle spoon, St. John, London, 1612. $1,190 £530

Early 17th century Swedish parcel gilt spoon, by Peter Povdsen, Va, circa 1610. $1,350 £600

16th century Maidenhead spoon. $1,485 £660

Rare Scottish disc-end spoon, by John Kirkwood, Glasgow, circa 1600. $1,485 £660

One of twelve George II Hanoverian pattern tablespoons, by M. Daintrey, London, 1739, 26oz.19dwt. $1,530 £680

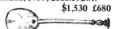

17th century silver gilt provincial baluster seal top spoon, by Jasper Radcliffe, Exeter, circa 1640. $1,610 £715

Rare 15th century French spoon, by Simon Lefevre, Paris. $1,600 £710

Elizabeth I seal top spoon, 1583. $1,630 £725

17th century apostle spoon, St. Matthias, Exeter. $1,645 £730

Silver spoon slipped in conventional manner and initialled on the slant B over I over A, London mark for 1649. $1,690 £750

Early silver spoon, probably English, Roman occupation or Anglo-Saxon period. $1,125 £500

One of a pair of 16th century seal top spoons, possibly Leicester.$1,755 £780

17th century St. Matthew apostle spoon, Exeter, circa 1650, maker's mark I.P. $1,755 £780

Mid 17th century parcel gilt and niello spoon, 19.5cm. long, 65gm.$2,195 £975

Elizabeth I Maidenhead spoon, London, 1602. $2,365 £1,050

One of two James I apostle spoons, London, 1605. $3,715 £1,650

Very rare Charles I horse's hoof terminal spoon. $4,500 £2,000

Early 17th century Barnstaple spoon, circa 1600. $4,500 £2,000

Maidenhead spoon, circa 1485. $4,725 £2,100

Charles II silver spoon with rare boar's head finial. $7,650 £3,400

Rare Mary I baluster knop spoon. $7,875 £3,500

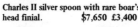

Early 16th century apostle's spoon, St. Philip. $9,000 £4,000

Berry top spoon, by P. Honnoure, Rouen, circa 1408. $9,450 £4,200

Silver apostle spoon showing St. Philip and enlarged London hallmark for 1490. $15,300 £6,800

One of a set of twelve silver gilt spoons, made in 1592. $225,000 £100,000

Silver mounted coconut shell goblet, 33cm. high, 402gm. **$1,900 £845**

One of a pair of silver gilt German goblets, 17th century. **$6,300 £2,800**

Mid 17th century silver wine goblet, 6in. high, 6oz.9dwt. **$12,375 £5,500**

HONEY POTS

George III 'Skep' honey pot and stand, London, 1798-1800, 12oz.17dwt., 4¾in. high. **$1,350 £600**

George III honey pot and stand, by Paul Storr. **$5,175 £2,300**

George III silver gilt honey pot, cover and stand, by Paul Storr, 4¾in. high, 1798, 14oz.8dwt. **$6,525 £2,900**

George III silver gilt honey pot, by Paul Storr, London, 1798, 12cm. high, 13oz. **$7,650 £3,400**

Silver gilt honey pot and matched stand, by Paul Storr, 1798, 4¾in. high, 14oz. **$8,440 £3,750**

George III silver honey pot and stand, by Paul Storr, 1797, 14oz.**$9,450 £4,200**

George II oblong inkstand, by Samuel Herbert & Co., London, 1759, 6¾in. wide, 9oz.4dwt. $990 £440

Two-bottle silver inkstand, by Burrage Davenport, London, 1777, 4in. long, 4oz. $1,240 £550

George II rectangular inkstand, by Samuel Herbert & Co., London, 1758, 9¾in. wide, 20oz.8dwt. $1,295 £575

George III oblong inkstand, 8in. wide, by Susanna Barker, London, 1770, 20oz. 7dwt. $1,620 £720

Simple Queen Anne silver inkstand. $2,140 £950

George II inkstand, by Robert Innes, 1745, 9¾in. long. $2,590 £1,150

Fine George II silver gilt inkstand, circa 1750, 12in. wide. $6,750 £3,000

George II rectangular inkstand, 9¾in. wide, by William Shaw, London, 1730, 24oz.16dwt. $14,065 £6,250

George III baluster silver jug with embossed decoration. $845 £375

George II silver baluster jug, 12½oz., 11.5cm. high. $1,070 £475

George II Irish, covered jug, 9¾in. high, by Andrew Goodwin, Dublin, circa 1747, 41oz.8dwt. $2,140 £950

18th century Spanish silver jug, 1762, 23.5cm. high, 750gm. $2,195 £975

Silver jug, by Abraham Pootholt and Jan van Giffen, 6in. high, 1784. $4,500 £2,000

Tiger-ware jug with Elizabeth I silver gilt mounts, 8½in. high, circa 1580. $5,400 £2,400

Jug with Elizabethan silver mounts, circa 1585, 9½in. high. $12,420 £5,520

Early Elizabeth I stoneware jug with silver gilt mountings, 7¼in. high, London, 1570. $25,875 £11,500

One of a pair of silver gilt jugs, by John Bache, 1705, 11¼in. high. $49,500 £22,000

George II baluster beer jug, 9¼in. high, by Wm. Shaw and Wm. Priest, London, 1752, 34oz. $5,175 £2,300

George I covered beer jug, by John Edwards, London, 1719, 10in. high, 32oz. 19dwt. $5,625 £2,500

18th century baluster shaped silver beer jug, by I.M. $5,625 £2,500

George II baluster beer jug, 8½in. high, by Thos. Coffin, Exeter, 1734, 28oz.7dwt. $5,625 £2,500

A very fine silver baluster beer jug, by Edward Feline, London, 1740. $5,625 £2,500

Early George III baluster beer jug, by Benjamin Cartwright, London, 1765, 7½in. high, 25oz.7dwt. $6,525 £2,900

George I large baluster beer jug, 10½in. high, by Thos. Folkingham, London, 1720, 42oz. 9dwt. $6,525 £2,900

George III beer jug and three mugs, by Thomas Moore II, London, 1759, 75oz.2dwt. $6,750 £3,000

George II baluster shaped silver beer jug, by Wm. Darker, London, 1730, 25oz. $6,750 £3,000

Georgian silver flat-bottomed cream jug, London, 1796. $205 £90

George III helmet-shaped cream jug, 5¾in. high, London, 1793, 3oz.13dwt. $505 £225

George III cream pail, by Wm. Vincent, London, 1774, 3¾in. high, 1oz.16dwt. $675 £300

George II circular cream jug, by Thos. Sutton, Dublin, 1735, 3¼in. high, 4oz.10dwt. $1,070 £475

18th century Dutch cow creamer, 7¾in. long. $1,190 £530

Oval body creamboat, by Christian Hilland, London, 1738, 5oz.19dwt., 4¾in. wide. $1,465 £650

George III cow creamer, by John Kentember, London, 1770, 5¾in. long, 4oz. $2,815 £1,250

George I pitcher cream jug, by Mungo Yorstoun, 1714, 7oz.17dwt., 4½in. high. $3,715 £1,650

George III silver cow creamer, 5¾in. long, by John Schuppe, 1765, 5oz.12dwt. $3,715 £1,650

Oval bodied cream jug, by Paul de Lamerie, London, 1740, 5¼in. wide, 6oz.11dwt. $3,940 £1,750

Early George III silver gilt cow creamer, by John Schuppe, London, 1763, 5½in. long, 3oz.16dwt. $5,175 £2,300

Baluster shaped cream jug and cover, Paris, 1753, 10.5cm. high, 185gm. $5,290 £2,350

67

Vase-shaped fluted coffee jug, by Ambrose Boxwell, Dublin, circa 1775, 27½oz. $1,630 £725

George III vase-shaped coffee jug, 13in. high, London, 1794, 24oz. 6dwt. $1,675 £745

George III silver coffee jug, engraved with a racing scene, by C. Wright, London, 1780. $1,800 £800

George III baluster coffee jug, by Henry Greenway, London, 1776, 12¼in. high, 25oz.10dwt. $1,845 £820

George III baluster coffee jug, by Daniel Smith and Robert Sharp, London, 1773, 11in. high, 25oz. 9dwt. $2,475 £1,100

George III vase-shaped coffee jug, by G. Smith, 1790, 12¼in. high, 28oz. 3dwt. $2,590 £1,150

George III coffee jug, by Paul Storr, London, 1792, 10in. high, 16oz.16dwt. $3,095 £1,375

18th century Maltese baluster coffee jug, by Gio. Carlo Cassar, 12¾in. high, 45oz.6dwt. $4,500 £2,000

18th century baluster shaped silver coffee jug, 7in. high, 11.9oz. $4,500 £2,000

Mid 18th century Irish milk jug, 4¼in. high, Dublin, 4oz. 15dwt. $620 £275

George III helmet-shaped milk jug, by Robert Sharp, London, 1793, 5in. high, 7oz.8dwt. $765 £340

George II Newcastle milk jug, 4½in. high, by Wm. Whitfield, 1742, 4oz. 19dwt. $865 £385

Swiss milk jug, 7¾in. high, Lausanne, 1800, 12oz. 16dwt. $900 £400

George III milk jug, by Hester Bateman, London, 1777, 6½in. high, 6oz. 12dwt. $1,045 £465

George II helmet-shaped milk jug, Dublin, circa 1748, 8oz., 4½in. high. $1,350 £600

George I hot milk jug, 4¾in. high, by S. Margas, London, 1717, 5oz.3dwt. $2,475 £1,100

George III Scottish provincial covered milk jug, by John Baillie, Inverness, circa 1780, 4¾in. high, 8oz. 4dwt. $2,700 £1,200

Baluster shaped milk jug and cover, stamped on the base, by Jacques-Pierre Marteau, Paris, 1763, 180gm. $2,880 £1,280

George III hot water jug,
London, 1775, 8in. high,
13oz. $370 £165

George III hot water jug,.
by Thos. Wynn, London,
1777, 26oz., 11in. high.
        $675 £300

George III baluster hot
water jug, by Charles
Wright, London, 1777,
13oz.12dwt.$1,050 £465

George III silver hot water
jug, 11¾in. high, by John
Scofield, London, 1785,
24oz. $1,915 £530

Silver topped shaving brush
and covered hot water jug,
by John Holloway, 1788.
        $3,490 £1,550

A fine Hester Bateman
baluster hot water jug, 1783.
        $4,500 £2,000

WINE

George II Irish, covered
jug, by Erasmus Cope,
Dublin, 1736, 33oz.8dwt.
        $5,625 £2,500

17th century Spanish silver
jug, with engraved gilt band
and mask beak spout,
24.5oz. $5,625 £2,500

Queen Anne Irish wine jug,
by Thos. Boulton of Dublin,
1702. $22,500 £10,000

LADLES

Georgian silver ladle, by George Smith and Wm. Fearn, London, 1790.
$100 £45

Fluted silver punch ladle, by E. Aldridge, 1742.
$360 £160

Silver soup ladle, by Hester Bateman, 1782.
$430 £190

LEMON STRAINERS

George I silver lemon strainer, Francis Nelme, London, 1727.
$450 £200

George III lemon strainer, by Hester Bateman, London, 1777, 4in. diam., 2oz.17dwt.
$900 £400

Large silver strainer, by Robert Calderwood, Dublin, 1752, 11½in. long.
$1,125 £500

LADLES

Bright cut ladle, by R. Keay, Perth, 1790.
$170 £75

Early George II punch ladle, by John Gamon, 1731, 12¾in. long.
$400 £180

One of a pair of George II Hanoverian pattern sauce ladles, by Elias Cachart, London, 1744, 5oz.5dwt. $720 £320

Silver lemon strainer, by H. Northcote, 1799.
$505 £225

George I lemon strainer, 6½in. wide, London, 1718, 3oz.2dwt. $955 £425

Early 18th century silver lemon strainer, by Thos. Bamford, 6in. long, 2oz.4dwt.
$1,520 £675

MISCELLANEOUS

Decorated and silver mounted nautilus shell, late 17th century. $7,425 £3,300

Queen Anne parcel gilt stand for a rimmon, by John Ruslen, 1708.
$1,350 £600

Early George III wax jack, 6¼in. high, by Samuel Herbert & Co., London, 1761, 5oz.9dwt.$900 £400

Scottish horn mull with silver mounts, 8¾in. long, circa 1760.$675 £300

Silver gilt travelling canteen by Thos. Heming and Robt. Garrard, 101oz.
$45,000 £20,000

Rare George III pastille burner, by A. Fogelberg and S. Gilbert, London, 1785, 7¾in. high, 9oz.17dwt.
$3,150 £1,400

Silver gilt model of a dromedary, probably by C. Erhard, Augsburg, circa 1600, 8½in. high. $33,750 £15,000

One of a pair of William III wall sconces, by M. Stockar, 1701, 30oz.
$101,250 £45,000

Silver figure of the Infant Lambrecht III, circa 1650, 25.8in. high.
$130,500 £60,000

Silver gilt mounted mother-of-pearl scissor case, circa 1700. $180 £80

George III dish cross, 12in. wide, by Robt. Hennell, London, 1782; 14oz.16dwt. $1,350 £600

Late 18th century pair of cockfighting spurs, 1¾in. long. $395 £175

Late 16th century silver gilt pomander, European, 2½in. high.$5,065 £2,250

One of a rare pair of George III silver spurs, London, 1784, maker B.C. $560 £250

16th century Spanish silver parcel gilt crucifix figure, 8in. long. $1,215 £540

Silver decanter stand, by John Scofield, circa 1790 $785 £350

George I censer, by Anthony Nelme, London, 1722, 8¾in. high, 27oz. 1dwt. $3,040 £1,350

Silver penny of King Offa's queen, Cynethryth, circa 787-792.$22,500 £10,000

73

MUGS

George III silver christening mug, London, 1798, by John Emes, 3oz.$315 £140

George II silver mug, London, 1752, by Robert Cox, 7.5oz. $395 £175

George III tapering cylindrical mug, 3¼in. high, by John Emes, London, 1799, 8oz. 4dwt. $520 £230

Queen Anne silver mug, London, 1711, 3¼oz. $540 £240

Baluster shaped silver mug, 1752. $585 £260

Silver mug, by John Langlands, Newcastle, 1769, 9oz., 11.5cm. high. $720 £320

George III silver pint baluster mug, by John Deacon, 1769, 5in. high, 10½oz. $865 £385

Large George III mug, by Henry Chawner, London, 1792, 22oz. $900 £400

George III tapered cylindrical mug, by John Scofield, London, 1791, 6in. high, 28oz.2dwt. $925 £410

George II baluster mug, 4¾in. high, by Fuller White, London, 1753, 12oz.19dwt. $970 £430

One of a pair of George III Scottish mugs, 4in. high, by P. Robertson, Edinburgh, 1777, 16oz. 16dwt. $1,070 £475

George II baluster mug, by Richard Bayley, London, 1738, 4½in. high, 12oz. $1,350 £600

George I tapering cylindrical mug, 4½in. high, by H. Payne, London, 1723, 11oz. 7dwt. $1,405 £625

Charles II tapering cylindrical mug, by Jonah Kirk, London, 1683, 9oz. 8dwt., 4in. high. $1,485 £660

William and Mary baluster mug, 3¼in. high, London, 1691, 4oz.18dwt. $1,610 £715

One of a pair of 18th century silver Channel Islands christening mugs. $1,630 £725

One of a pair of George III baluster mugs, 4½in. high, 19oz.11dwt. $1,690 £750

Charles II baluster mug, London, 1683, 5oz.17dwt. $1,690 £750

MUGS

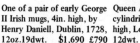

One of a pair of early George II Irish mugs, 4in. high, by Henry Daniell, Dublin, 1728, 12oz.19dwt. $1,690 £790

Queen Anne tapering cylindrical mug, 4¾in. high, London, 1712, 9oz. 12dwt. $1,755 £780

One of a pair of George II Irish mugs, by Michael Fowler, Dublin, circa 1750, 4in. high, 16oz.18dwt. $2,250 £1,000

William III cylindrical mug, by John Fawdery I, London, 1698, 9oz., 3¼in. high. $2,590 £1,150

Queen Anne plain covered mug, 4¼in. high, by John Chartier, 1703, 8oz.15dwt. $3,600 £1,600

William and Mary baluster mug, 5¼in. high, London, 11oz.19dwt. $4,050 £1,800

One of a pair of George II silver mugs, 4in. high, by Richard Gurney & Co., London, 1745, 22oz.9dwt. $4,500 £2,000

A pair of George I Scottish mugs, 3in. high, by Mungo Yorstoun, Edinburgh, 1717, 11oz.15dwt. $5,175 £2,300

An exceptionally fine Paul de Lamerie silver mug, 1727, 14½oz. $5,625 £2,500

Italian mustard pot and stand, Naples, 1792, stand 4½in. diam., 7oz.10dwt. $385 £170

Mustard pot and caster en suite, late 18th century, 6¼in. high, 11oz. 12dwt. $565 £250

George III vase-shaped mustard pot, 5in. high, by Robt. Hennell I, London, 1790, and spoon, 5oz. 1dwt. $565 £250

George III barrel-shaped mustard pot, by Robert and David Hennell, London, 1798, 3in. high, 3oz.13dwt. $765 £340

A pierced mustard pot by Robert Hennell, London, 1783. $900 £400

George III cylindrical mustard pot, by Hester Bateman, 1790, with spoon, 3½in. high, 3oz. 8dwt. $1,015 £450

George III mustard pot, by Hester Bateman, London, 1783, 3oz.8dwt. $1,690 £750

George I octagonal caster and dry mustard pot, 4½in. high, London, 1722, 5oz.13dwt. $2,475 £1,100

One of a rare pair of early George III openwork mustard pots, by A. Le Sage, London, 1765, 7oz.19dwt., 2¾in. high. $3,600 £1,600

NUTMEGS

George III silver nutmeg grater, by Mary Hyde and John Reily, London, 1799, 2in. diam. **$225 £100**

Rare Sheffield plated cylindrical nutmeg grater case with grater inside, about 1790. **$225 £100**

Late 18th century egg-shaped nutmeg grater, by Samuel Meriton. **$450 £200**

Georgian silver nutmeg grater, by Phipps & Robinson, London, 1788, 2¾in. high. **$565 £250**

George III oval nutmeg grater, by Phipps & Robinson, London, 1786, 2¼in. wide. **$700 £310**

George III silver gilt oval memorial nutmeg grater, 2in. wide, by John Reily, London, 1793. **$1,180 £525**

PAP BOATS

Georgian silver pap boat, maker's mark TE, 4¼in., 2oz. **$170 £75**

Unmarked silver and coconut shell pap boat, circa 1760, 5in. long. **$170 £75**

George III silver pap boat, by Rebecca Emes and Edward Barnard, 2½oz. **$325 £145**

George I cylindrical kitchen pepper, by John Hamilton, Dublin, 2½in. high, 2oz.9dwt.
$820 £365

George I octagonal kitchen pepper, by Glover Johnson, London, 1726, 2oz.16dwt., 3¾in. high.
$855 £380

George I kitchen pepper, 3¼in. high, London, 1724, 2oz.1dwt. $1,180 £525

PLATES

George I Irish circular plate, 9in. diam., Dublin, 1725, 13oz.13dwt.
$2,475 £1,100

One of twelve George III shaped circular dinner plates, 9¾in. diam., by L. Herne and F. Butty, London, 1762, 212oz.15dwt.
$7,875 £3,500

One of twelve George II dinner plates, 9¾in. diam., by G. Methuen, London, 1756, 196oz.6dwt.
$7,875 £3,500

One of twelve George I dinner plates, 9¼in. diam., by E. Cornock, London, 1724-25, 219oz.
$14,065 £6,250

One of a set of twelve William III plain circular dinner plates, by Phillip Rollos, 1701, 235oz.
$16,875 £7,500

Silver charger, by Louis Mettayer, London, 1720, 68cm. diam., 234oz.
$22,500 £10,000

PORRINGERS

George II silver porringer, by Sarah Parr, London, 1731, 10oz. $540 £240

Queen Anne porringer on collet foot, 1713, 6oz. $620 £275

Late 17th century provincial porringer, 2¾in. high, 4oz. 4dwt. $720 £320

17th century design silver porringer. $730 £325

Late 18th century porringer, 4¾in. diam., 6oz. 19dwt. $745 £330

Queen Anne porringer, 4in. high, by Robt. Peake, London, 1708, 8oz.17dwt. $1,125 £500

Queen Anne silver porringer, by John Wisdome, London, 1706, 4oz., 2¾in. high. $1,215 £540

William III porringer, by James Chadwick, London, 1697, 3¼in. high, 6oz. $1,240 £550

Queen Anne porringer, 4½in. high, by Thomas Parr I, London, 1704, 9oz.9dwt. $1,350 £600

80

William III porringer, by S. Lofthouse, London, 1700, 6¾in. wide, 7oz.4dwt.
$1,530 £680

Charles II porringer, 3in. high, 7oz.4dwt.
$1,620 £720

James II porringer, 3¼in. high, by Y.T., London, 1688, 6oz. $1,755 £780

Charles II plain silver gilt porringer, 3½in. high, 7oz. 7dwt. $1,800 £800

Commonwealth porringer, by Gilbert Shepherd, London, 1656, 2in. high, 2oz.8dwt. $2,025 £900

Commonwealth porringer, 3½in. high, London, 1659, 10oz.3dwt. $2,115 £940

17th century provincial porringer, 3in. high, by Wm. Clare, Warminster, circa 1685, 5oz.3dwt.
$2,140 £950

One of a pair of Queen Anne porringers, by John East, London, 1707, 16oz.16dwt., 4in. high. $2,365 £1,050

Charles II two-handled porringer, 4½in. high, 13oz. 13dwt. $2,475 £1,100

Commonwealth two-handled porringer and cover, 3¾in. high, 1659, 5oz.12dwt. $2,700 £1,200

Commonwealth two-handled porringer, 1652, maker's mark I.H., 9.2cm. high. $2,815 £1,250

Charles II silver porringer, by R.A., London, 1663, 14oz. $2,815 £1,250

Charles II plain two-handled porringer on rim foot, probably West Country, maker's mark IP, circa 1670, 6oz. 3dwt. $3,825 £1,700

Mid 17th century porringer by N. Wollaston, London, 1650, 6in. wide, 7oz. 10dwt. $4,165 £1,850

One of a pair of George II Scottish provincial porringers, 3in. high, by James Glen, Glasgow, circa 1745, 15oz.1dwt. $5,175 £2,300

Charles II two-handled porringer and cover, 6in. high, 1661, 20oz. $5,400 £2,400

Charles II porringer, London, 1674, 22½oz. $6,190 £2,750

Rare Charles II silver gilt porringer and cover, 1670, 29oz. $108,000 £48,000

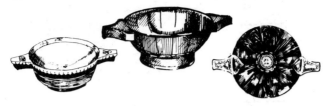

Silver mounted wood quaich,
4½in. diam., circa 1720.
                $565 £250

George II two-handled
quaich, 5in. diam., by
Alex. Kincaid, Edinburgh,
5oz.11dwt. $2,250 £1,000

A typical Stuart quaich,
7¾in. diam., unmarked,
Scottish, circa 1675.
                $3,040 £1,350

Queen Anne quaich, by Robt.
Ker, Edinburgh, circa 1710.
                $3,490 £1,550

Silver quaich, circa 1700,
5¾in. wide, 9½oz.
                $4,500 £2,000

George I quaich, Edinburgh,
1721, assay master Edward
Penman, 20.4cm. long,
29oz. $11,250 £5,000

RATTLES

18th century child's rattle
and whistle, by Shem
Drowne, Boston, 1740.
                $550 £245

Early 18th century child's
silver rattle, 5¼in. long,
circa 1700. $810 £360

17th century child's rattle
bearing the Edinburgh date
letter for 1681.
                $2,815 £1,250

83

George III pierced salt, by Fenton Creswick & Co., Sheffield, 1776. $190 £85

One of a pair of George III silver salts of spool-shape, London, 1792, 6oz. $190 £85

One of a pair of Irish George III silver salts. $295 £130

One of a pair of silver boat-shaped salts, James Young, London, 1787. $450 £200

One of a pair of circular silver salts, by Hester Bateman, London, 1774. $565 £250

One of a set of four George III oval pierced salts by David R. Hennell, 1765. $600 £265

One of a pair of George III silver gilt oval salt cellar stands, 4in. wide, by Saml. Roberts, Jnr., Sheffield, 1800. $620 £275

One of a pair of late 18th century Dutch salt cellars, by R. Sondag, Rotterdam, 1780, 4oz.17dwt. $640 £285

One of a pair of late 18th century silver gilt salts, complete with spoons, 23oz. $845 £375

One of a pair of George III salt cellars, by Edward Wood, London, 2¾in. diam., 11oz.7dwt. $900 £400

One of a pair of 18th century Italian trencher salt cellars, 3¼in. wide, 6oz. 18dwt. $1,015 £450

One of a pair of Queen Anne trencher salt cellars, by B. Bentley, 3in. diam., 4oz.2dwt. $1,350 £600

One of a set of four George III double salts, 4¼in. wide, by J. Scofield, London, 1784, 28oz.15dwt.
$1,630 £725

George I silver kitchen salt, by Wm. Darkeratt, London, 1726.
$1,860 £825

One of a pair of George II trencher salts, by Edward Wood, London, 1724, 4oz. 15dwt.　$1,860 £825

One of a set of six George III salt cellars, 4¾in. wide, by D. Smith and R. Sharp, London, 1785, 28oz.18dwt.
$2,700 £1,200

One of a pair of silver salts, by Paul Storr, 1810.
$2,815 £1,250

One of a set of four George II capstan salts, London, 1754, by G. Wickes, 32oz.
$2,925 £1,300

One of a set of four George II circular salt cellars, by Peter Taylor, London, 1740, 18oz.15dwt. $3,040 £1,350

One of a pair of early 18th century Danish trencher salts, 3¼in. wide, by G. Bolch, Copenhagen, 1708, 6oz.
$3,150 £1,400

Early 17th century Spanish standing salt, 8½in. high, 21oz.2dwt. $3,600 £1,600

One of a set of four silver trencher salts, by John Cole, 1706.
$2,475 £1,900

One of a set of six George II shell-shaped salt cellars, by P. Archambo I, 1744, 41oz.　$6,190 £2,750

One of a set of eight silver salts, by Paul Storr.
$33,750 £15,000

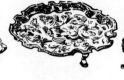

18th century oblong silver salver on scroll feet, by Gravenhage, circa 1775, 9½oz. $335 £150

George II silver salver, by Ebenezer Coker and Thos. Hannay, London, 1759, 11½oz., 19.5cm. diam. $385 £170

An oval silver salver on scroll feet, by Hester Bateman, London, 1790, 4½oz. $620 £275

George II shaped circular waiter, 5½in. diam., by E. Feline, London, 1733, 7oz.3dwt. $675 £300

George II triangular salver by George Methuen, London, 1752, 16oz.4dwt. 9½in. wide. $810 £360

George III circular salver, by John Scofield, London, 1777, 13oz.17dwt. $810 £360

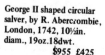

George III salver by David Willaume, 1742, 10¾in. diam., 24½oz. $810 £360

George II shaped circular salver, by R. Abercrombie, London, 1742, 10½in. diam., 19oz.18dwt. $955 £425

George III shaped circular salver, 11¼in. diam., by J. Carter, London, 1773, 24oz.2dwt. $970 £430

George IH shaped circular salver, by Elizabeth Cooke, London, 1766, 12in. diam., 29oz.15dwt. $970 £430

George II Scottish provincial waiter, 6in. diam., by George Cooper, Aberdeen, circa 1730, 6oz. 4dwt. $1,080 £480

One of a pair of George III shaped circular salvers, 7in. diam., by J. Carter, London, 1767, 18oz.4dwt. $1,125 £500

George III shaped circular salver, by Robt. Abercrombie, London, 1739, 19oz.15dwt., 10¼in. diam. $1,125 £500

George II plain shaped circular salver on rim foot, by Wm. Aytoun, Edinburgh, 1733, 11oz. 14dwt. $1,170 £520

One of a pair of George III circular salvers, by Crouch & Hannam, London, 1777, 19oz.14dwt., 7¼in. diam. $1,195 £530

One of a pair of George II shaped circular salvers, by Isaac Cookson, Newcastle, 1756, 21oz.6dwt., 7¼in. diam. $1,235 £550

Early George III shaped circular salver, 14½in. diam., by Robert Rew, 1762, 39oz.4dwt. $1,295 £575

George II circular shaped salver, by Wm. Peaston, London, 1753, 10¾in. diam., 18oz.19dwt. $1,305 £580

87

One of a pair of George II waiters, by J. Robinson, London, 1745, 14oz.6dwt.
$1,385 £615

One of a pair of George III shaped silver salvers, 8in. square, by Wakelin & Taylor, London, 1785, 23oz.8dwt.$1,405 £625

One of two Irish waiters on foot, 5in. diam., by Robt. Calderwood and John Moore, Dublin, circa 1730-40, 11oz.2dwt.
$1,425 £635

George III shaped circular salver, 13¾in. diam., by R. Makepeace and R. Carter, London, 1777, 39oz.8dwt.
$1,485 £660

One of a pair of George I Irish waiters on foot, 5in. diam., by P. Kinnersley, Dublin, 1717, 9oz.11dwt.
$1,485 £660

George III circular salver, by Elizabeth Cooke, London, 1771, 11½in. diam., 35oz.2dwt.$1,540 £685

George II square-shaped salver, by John Tuite, London, 1730, 24oz., 10½in. wide.
$1,540 £685

George III shaped circular salver by Boulton & Fothergill, Birmingham, 15in. diam., 1775, 47oz. 18dwt. $1,575 £700

George III circular salver, 12¾in. diam., by John Carter, London, 1774, 32oz. 5dwt. $1,575 £700

George III circular salver, by Crouch & Hannam, London, 1798, 49oz. 3dwt., 15in. diam.
$1,610 £715

One of a pair of George II shaped circular salvers, by Edward Wakelin, London, 1752, 7in. diam., 22oz.12dwt.**$1,610 £715**

One of a pair of George II circular waiters, by J. Sanders, London, 1734, 15oz.10dwt., 6¼in. diam.
$1,675 £745

One of a pair of Irish provincial waiters on foot, 5in. diam., by Wm. Clarke, Cork, 1730, 10oz.14dwt.
$1,845 £820

Early George III circular salver, 15½in. diam., by E. Coker, London, 1768, 52oz.9dwt. **$1,890 £840**

George I Irish silver circular salver on domed foot, 1714, 13¼oz., 8½in. diam.
$2,025 £900

George III shaped circular salver, by Richard Rugg II, London, 1775, 44oz.13dwt., 14¼in. diam. **$2,205 £980**

George II shaped circular salver, by Wm. Peaston, London, 1751, 13½in. diam., 37oz.14dwt.
$2,250 £1,000

George II silver salver, by John Tuite, London, 1738, 30oz. **$2,360 £1,050**

Maltese shaped circular salver, 11¼in. diam., circa 1780, 31oz. $2,590 £1,150

Square silver salver, 9½in., 25oz.3dwt., by Abraham Buteux, 1726. $3,150 £1,400

George II plain circular salver, by John Swift, 1739, 21oz., 10½in. diam. $3,375 £1,500

Fine Queen Anne circular salver, on foot, Dublin, 1712-14. $3,600 £1,600

Early 18th century Dutch octafoil salver, 14oz.13dwt., 9½in. diam., by Jacques Tuillier, The Hague, 1721. $4,275 £1,900

George II large shaped circular salver, by G. Hindmarsh, 1739, 171oz. $5,175 £2,300

George II plain shaped square silver salver, by Robert Abercrombie. $5,175 £2,300

George II shaped circular salver, by Peter Archambo, 1740, 20¾in. diam. $7,315 £3,250

George II shaped square salver, by Edward Cornock, London, 1728, 13in. square, 44oz.16dwt. $21,375 £9,500

One of a pair of mid 18th century sauceboats, London, 37oz.17dwt., rubbed marks. $1,690 £750

One of a pair of George II plain oval sauceboats, by Thos. Heming, 1756, 23oz. $1,690 £750

One of a pair of George III silver sauceboats, by W. Quipps, 8in. wide, 22oz. $1,800 £800

One of a pair of 18th century silver sauceboats, London, 1770. $1,855 £825

One of a pair of George II oval sauceboats, 8in. wide, 30oz.6dwt. $1,855 £825

One of a pair of George III silver sauceboats, 1780, by Wm. Skeen. $1,855 £825

George III oval sauceboat, by Hester Bateman, London, 1783, 7oz.19dwt. $1,855 £825

One of a pair of George III Scottish sauceboats, by F. Howden, Edinburgh, 1788, 20oz.16dwt. $1,890 £840

One of a pair of George II Irish sauceboats, 27oz. 10dwt. $1,945 £865

One of a pair of George III oval sauceboats, by Wm. Skeen, London, 1769, 20oz 12dwt., 6¾in. wide. $1,970 £875

One of a pair of George III oval sauceboats, London, 1770, 16oz.15dwt., 6¾in. wide. $2,250 £1,000

One of a pair of early George III oval sauceboats, by Wm. Skeen, London, 1763, 8¼in. wide, 29oz. 12dwt. $2,365 £1,050

91

One of a pair of George III oval sauceboats, by Thos. Evans, London, 1775, 34oz. 7dwt., 7½in. wide. $2,475 £1,100

One of a pair of George III Irish oval sauceboats, by Joseph Nixon, Dublin, circa 1770, 25oz.8dwt. $2,475 £1,100

One of two George II sauceboats, by Peter Archambo, London, 29oz.7dwt. $2,590 £1,150

One of a pair of George III mint sauceboats, 1774, maker George Smith. $2,925 £1,300

One of a pair of George III double lidded sauceboats, 36oz. $3,040 £1,350

One of a pair of George III oval sauceboats, 8½in., by Sebastion and James Crespell, London, 1763, 32oz.3dwt. $3,040 £1,350

One of a pair of George III sauceboats, by G. Smith, London, 1770, 6¾in. long, 16oz.16dwt.$3,150 £1,400

One of a pair of George II sauceboats, by John Pollock, London, 1754, 8¼in. long, 26oz.7dwt. $3,375 £1,500

One of a pair of George II oval sauceboats, 8¼in., by Edward Wakelin, London, 1750, 37oz.15dwt. $3,490 £1,550

One of a pair of George III oval sauceboats, 8in. wide, 27oz.12dwt. $3,600 £1,600

One of a pair of George III plain oval sauceboats, by Alex. Johnston, 1763, 30oz. $3,715 £1,650

One of a pair of George III small sauceboats, by F. White, London, 1758, 10oz. 17dwt. $3,940 £1,750

One of a pair of 18th century sauceboats, 8in. wide, circa 1740, 36oz.12dwt.
$4,050 £1,800

One of a pair of George III oval sauceboats, 7in., by Walter Brind, London, 1784, 24oz.7dwt.
$4,390 £1,950

One of a pair of George II oval sauceboats, by Wm. Cripps, London, 1754, 8in. wide, 28oz.8dwt.
$4,390 £1,950

One of a pair of George II oval sauceboats, by Chas. Martin, London, 1732, 17oz.11dwt.
$4,725 £2,100

One of a pair of George III plain oval sauceboats, by James Young, 1771, 30oz.
$5,175 £2,300

One of a pair of George II oval sauceboats, by Wm. Grundy, 1744, 35oz.
$5,400 £2,400

One of a pair of George II sauceboats, by F. White, 1747, 34oz. $5,400 £2,400

One of a pair of silver sauceboats, by Paul de Lamerie, 1748.
$7,200 £3,200

One of a pair of George II oval sauceboats, by Paul de Lamerie, London, 1750, 43oz.9dwt., 8½in. high.
$7,315 £3,250

One of a set of four George III plain oval sauceboats, 1763, 63oz. $7,540 £3,350

One of a pair of Dutch oval sauceboats, 8in. long, by Francois van Stapele, 1785, 26oz. 19dwt. $8,440 £3,750

One of a pair of George II oval double lipped sauceboats, by Thos. Farrer, 1727. $9,000 £4,000

SCOOPS

A George II marrow scoop, probably by Robert Burton, London, 1759.
$180 £80

Silver marrow scoop, by Benjamin Godfrey, London, 1736. $180 £80

Silver marrow scoop, by E. B., London, 1745. $250 £110

Combined silver marrow scoop and table-spoon, by Elias Cachart, 1750. $395 £175

SKEWERS

Silver skewer, maker's mark rubbed, London, 1779. $90 £40

Silver meat skewer, by Thomas Wright, London, 1754. $180 £80

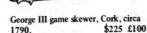

George III game skewer, Cork, circa 1790. $225 £100

Pair of silver meat skewers, by Peter and Ann Bateman, 1798. $225 £100

SNUFFERS

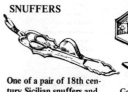

One of a pair of 18th century Sicilian snuffers and stands, by P. Donia, Messina, 11in. long, 6oz.8dwt.
$810 £360

George III Irish boat-shaped snuffers tray, by James Scott, Dublin, 8oz. 5dwt. $865 £385

Silver snuffers tray, by Paul de Lamerie, 1725, 7¼in. wide. $4,500 £2,000

Queen Anne snuffers stand and a pair of snuffers, by Thos. Prichard, London, 1704, 11oz.17dwt.
$5,625 £2,500

18th century Dutch silver snuffer stand and snuffers, by Jan Pondt of Bremen, Amsterdam, 1756, 9oz. 18dwt. $6,750 £3,000

Charles II snuffer tray with matching snuffers, by W.B., 15oz.12dwt.
$33,750 £15,000

Early 18th century Russian silver snuff box. $335 £150

Small English gilt metal snuff box, mid 18th century, Birmingham, 3.8cm. wide.$360 £160

Silver pocket snuff box, by Ambrose Stevenson, circa 1720. $395 £175

George II rectangular snuff box, 2½in. wide, London, 1732. $595 £265

George III silver snuff box, by Thos. Phipps and E. Robinson, London, 1791, 3in. long. $605 £270

English gilt metal snuff box, 2¾in. wide, circa 1740. $710 £315

French oval tortoiseshell pique snuff box, 3¾in. wide, Paris, 1760. $810 £360

George III Irish silver snuff box, by A. Tuppy, Dublin, 1782, 3¼in. wide. $880 £390

George II cartouche shaped snuff box, 2¼in. wide, London, 1743.$1,015 £450

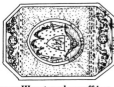

Early 18th century Boscobel oak silver snuff box, unmarked, circa 1700, 3¼in. wide. $1,180 £525

George III rectangular snuff box, 3in. wide, by Wm. Robertson, Edinburgh, circa 1790. $1,190 £530

Rare early 18th century Irish rectangular snuff box, by Robt. Goble, Cork, 3¼in. wide. $1,610 £715

Snuff box, by Hester Bateman, 1789, 3½in. long. $1,620 £720

French silver snuff box, Paris, 1730, 6.5cm. wide. $1,825 £810

Early 17th century Jacobite snuff box, 2¼in. diam., circa 1715. $1,915 £850

George II oblong snuff box, London, 1757, 2¾in. wide. $1,915 £850

Late 18th century polished and shell carved agate snuff box with gold mounts, 2½in. wide. $2,250 £1,000

18th century gold and enamel snuff box with lid painted by Richter. $3,940 £1,750

A rare late 18th century silver gilt 'mask' snuff box, 3in. wide. $5,625 £2,500

A mid 18th century English snuff box of pudding stone mounted in gold. $5,625 £2,500

Unusual silver gilt snuff box in the form of a book, by A. J. Strachan, London. $6,075 £2,700

Attractive Meissen snuff box with silver gilt mounts, circa 1735, 7cm. wide. $11,700 £5,200

Louis XVI octagonal gold snuff box, Paris, 1774, 8.3cm. wide. $18,000 £8,000

An 18th century French gold and enamel snuff box. $168,750 £75,000

George II baluster shaped silver tankard, 1732. $585 £260

George III barrel-shaped tankard, 6¾in. high, by G. Cowles, London, 1778, 29oz.8dwt. $900 £400

George II tankard, by R. Gurney & Co., London, 1740, 4¾in. high, 13oz. 10dwt. $1,180 £525

Early George III tankard, 8in. high, by W.F., London, 1767, 15oz.1dwt. $1,465 £650

Dutch silver mounted horn tankard with silver lining, with portrait of William and Mary on side. $1,575 £700

George III tankard, London, 1765, 7½in. high, 24½oz. $1,630 £725

George III tapering cylin-drical tankard, by Peter and Anne Bateman, Lon-don, 1797, 7¼in. high, 26oz.6dwt.$1,690 £750

Early 18th century silver tankard, by Nathaniel Lock, 22½oz. $1,800 £800

George II cylindrical tankard, by Richard Bell, London, 19oz.6dwt., 6½in. high. $1,970 £875

TANKARDS

George III baluster tankard, 8in. high, by Hester Bateman, London, 1780, 24oz.1dwt. $2,025 £900

George III baluster tankard, London, 1775, 30oz.8dwt., 8½in. high. $2,100 £935

George II baluster tankard, by Peter Moss, London, 1747, 8¼in. high, 27oz.3dwt. $2,100 £935

George II baluster tankard, by Richard Gosling, London, 1739, 28oz.16dwt. $2,250 £1,000

Queen Anne plain cylindrical tankard, 7in. high, by Anthony Nelme, 1705, 27oz. $2,590 £1,150

Queen Anne tapering cylindrical tankard, by J. Elston, Exeter, 1707, 16oz.1dwt., 6¼in. high. $2,590 £1,150

George III tapered cylindrical tankard, by Chas. Wright, London, 1778, 8in. high, 26oz.7dwt. $2,815 £1,250

Plain bodied silver tankard, by William Shaw, London, 1762, 27oz. $2,815 £1,250

Queen Anne cylindrical tankard, 8in. high, by Alice Sheene, London, 1709, 30oz. 8dwt. $3,040 £1,350

Charles II silver tankard, London, 1683, possibly by J. Buck, 6in. high, 21½oz.
$3,040 £1,350

Good Queen Anne cylindrical tankard, 6½in. high, by A. Stevenson, London, 1713, 22oz. 10dwt. $3,150 £1,400

George II plain cylindrical tankard, by John Swift, 1731, 40oz.$3,150 £1,400

One of a pair of George III tapering tankards, by Robt. Sharp, London, 1794, 64oz. 2dwt., 7¼in. high.
$3,150 £1,400

George II baluster tankard, by Richard Gosling, London, 1739, 29oz. 16dwt., 8in. high. $3,265 £1,450

William and Mary silver tankard, by I.C., London, 1689, 35oz. $3,600 £1,600

Queen Anne cylindrical tankard, 6in. high, by S. Lofthouse, London, 1702, 16oz.10dwt.$3,940 £1,750

Early George II cylindrical tankard, by R. Lucas, London, 1727, 38oz. 13dwt., 7½in. high.
$4,050 £1,800

George II baluster tankard, by F. White, London, 1759, 26oz.18dwt., 7¾in. high.
$4,165 £1,850

Queen Anne tapered cylindrical tankard, by J. Martin Stockar, London, 1712, 16oz.3dwt., 5¾in. high.
$4,275 £1,900

George III tankard, by Hester Bateman, 23½oz.
$4,275 £1,900

Queen Anne Irish tankard, 8in. high, by J. Walker, Dublin, 1706, 35oz.1dwt.
$4,500 £2,000

Silver tankard, by Robert Timbrell and Benjamin Bentley, 1714, 8¾in. high, 42oz.
$4,500 £2,000

George II tapered cylindrical tankard, by Thos. Farren, London, 1731, 7¼in. high, 31oz.11dwt.
$5,625 £2,500

Charles II tapering cylindrical tankard, London, 1678, 7¼in. high, 25oz.19dwt.
$6.750 £3,000

18th century Norwegian tankard, 9½in. high, circa 1750, 38oz.3dwt.
$7,200 £3,200

Silver Augsburg tankard, circa 1700, 33oz., with embossed decoration.
$7,425 £3,300

17th century German silver gilt tankard, 6¾in. high, 15oz.18dwt.
$7,875 £3,500

17th century German cylindrical tankard, 7¾in. high, 28oz.5dwt.$7,540 £3,350

James II tapering cylindrical tankard, by J. Jackson, London, 1688, 8¾in. high, 39oz.19dwt. $7,875 £3,500

One of a pair of George II silver quart tankards with lids, by Thos. Heming, London, 1746, 7½in. high, 68oz. $7,875 £3,500

17th century Norwegian tankard, 8in. high, 40oz. 6dwt. $8,665 £3,850

Charles II tapered cylindrical tankard, London, 1679, 25oz. $9,000 £4,000

Dutch plain tapering cylindrical tankard on domed foot, maker's mark IF, Groningen, 1705, 8oz. 13dwt. $9,000 £4,000

Charles II cylindrical tankard, by Marmaduke Best, York, 24oz.19dwt., 6½in. high. $10,350 £4,600

Massive parcel gilt cylindrical tankard, 9¼in. high, marked Danzig, 17th century. $10,800 £4,800

Charles II tapering cylindrical tankard, London, 1664, 6¼in. high, 21oz.3dwt. $11,250 £5,000

Large Charles II cylindrical tankard, 8¾in. high, by R. Leake, London, 1679, 50oz.6dwt.
$11,770 £5,230

Early 17th century Danish peg tankard, 7¼in. high, by M. Clausson, Copenhagen, circa 1610, 28oz.10dwt.
$13,500 £6,000

Late 17th century Austrian silver gilt and ivory covered beer tankard.
$14,065 £6,250

Fine rare lidded tankard, by Arthur Heaslewood, 23oz., 7in. high.
$15,750 £7,000

Norwegian cylindrical peg tankard on three pomegranate feet, Oslo, 1684, maker's mark RR or KK, 53oz.
$16,200 £7,200

James II peg tankard, 7½in. high, London, 1686, 27oz. 18dwt. $17,440 £7,750

Charles I tankard, by T.I., London, 1639, 29oz. 13dwt., 7¾in. high.
$20,250 £9,000

German parcel gilt tankard, by Melchior Gibb, circa 1620, 9½in. high.
$33,750 £15,000

Elizabethan silver gilt tankard, 8in. high, 19¾oz., maker's mark IR.
$56,250 £25,000

George II silver taperstick, by Wm. Shaw and Wm. Priest, 4½in. high.
$620 £275

Georgian taperstick, by E. Coker, London, 1759, 5½in. high, 6oz. 3dwt.$730 £325

George II taperstick, by Wm. Paradise, London, 1730, 3oz.3dwt., 4in. high.
$935 £415

A George I silver taperstick, by M. Cooper, London, 1717-18, 6oz., 4¾in. high.
$1,240 £550

Silver taperstick, by D. Green, London, 1722, 11cm. high.
$1,350 £600

George II taperstick, by J. Cafe, London, 1743, 4½in. high, 4oz. 7dwt.
$1,530 £680

Silver taperstick, by E. Barnet, York, 1713, 2¾oz.
$1,800 £800

One of a pair of early George III tapersticks, by E. Coker, London, 1760, 6in. high, 14oz.14dwt.
$4,165 £1,850

TAZZAS

18th century Dutch silver gilt tazza, by Casparus Janszonius Haarlem, 4¾in. diam., 3oz.14dwt.
$2,025 £900

Early 17th century Spanish tazza, 10in. wide, circa 1630, 19oz. $4,050 £1,800

Early 17th century Dutch tazza, 7in. high, 13oz. 12dwt. $9,000 £4,000

TEA CADDIES

Sheffield plate caddy, about 1775-80, with typical Adam decoration and a lock. $270 £120

A silver Portuguese tea caddy, by P.I.E., Porto, circa 1810. $785 £350

George II tea caddy, by S. Taylor, London, 1755, 5¼in. high, 7oz.16dwt. $955 £425

George III oval tea caddy, 5in. high, by Wm. Vincent, London, 1778, 3oz.10dwt. $1,015 £450

George III oblong tea caddy, by P. Gillois, London, 1763, 11oz. 7dwt., 5½in. high. $1,095 £485

George III tea caddy, by Wm. Vincent, London, 1778, 12½oz. $1,240 £550

George I tea caddy, 4¾in. high, by John Eckford, London, 1726, 6oz.15dwt. $1,350 £600

George III tea caddy, marked on base and cover, by Robt. Hennell, London, 1782, 4in. high, 13oz.2dwt.$1,350 £600

George III two-division tea caddy, by Daniel Pontifex, London, 1797, 19oz.13dwt., 7in. high. $1,350 £600

One of two matching tea caddies, by S. Herbert & Co., London, 1750-52, 15oz.18dwt.
$1,405 £625

George III oval tea caddy, by Wm. Vincent, London, 1785, 12oz.19dwt., 5½in. high. $1,485 £660

18th century Norwegian tea caddy, by Jens Kahrs, Bergen, 1765, 11.2cm. high.
$1,605 £715

George III cylindrical tea caddy, 4¾in. high, marked on base and lid by Augustin le Sage, London, 1767, 15oz.13dwt. $1,635 £725

Queen Anne octagonal tea caddy, 4½in. high, by Thos. Ash, London, 1713, 7oz.4dwt.
$1,690 £750

One of a pair of George II tea caddies, 5¼in. high, by S. Taylor, London, 1756, 16oz.2dwt.$1,750 £775

One of a pair of Georgian octagonal tea caddies, 4½in. high, by J. Farnell, London, 1721, 11oz.15dwt.
$1,915 £850

One of a pair of George II oblong tea caddies, by S. Taylor, London, 1755, 18oz.12dwt., 4¾in. high.
$2,250 £1,000

One of two George III tea caddies, by P. Gillois, London, 1760, 6in. high, 22oz. $2,250 £1,000

TEA CADDIES

George II bombe tea caddy, 5¾in. high, by J. Langford and J. Sebille, London, 1766, 10oz.13dwt.
$2,475 £1,100

Pair of early George III tea caddies in case, 6in. high, by John Langford II and John Sebille, London, 25oz. 11dwt. $2,475 £1,100

George III tea caddy, by Hester Bateman, 1779, 10.75oz.
$2,475 £1,100

18th century Dutch tea caddy, 5in. high, 4oz.10dwt., Rotterdam. $2,700 £1,200

Pair of tea caddies and a mixing bowl, by Samuel Taylor, London, 1755, 27oz.15dwt., in a veneered rosewood case. $2,700 £1,200

Dutch tea caddy, circa 1713, 3¾in. high, 3oz.10dwt.
$3,150 £1,400

George III oval tea caddy, by Hester Bateman, London, 1784, 10oz.18dwt., 5½in. high. $3,375 £1,500

George III square tea caddy, engraved with imitation Chinese characters, maker's mark AL, 1786, 14oz.7dwt. $3,375 £1,500

One of a pair of George II oval tea caddies, by John Farnell, London, 1727, 5in. high, 16oz.10dwt.
$3,600 £1,600

106

George III drum-shaped
tea caddy, by J. Vere
and Wm. Lutwyche,
London, 1768, 4in.
high, 15oz.9dwt.
$3,600 £1,600

Set of three George II rectangular
tea caddies, 4½in. high, by Paul
Crespin, London, 1743, 37oz.
$4,500 £2,000

One of a pair of
George I tea cad-
dies, 5in. high, by
G. Roode, London,
1715, 11oz.4dwt.
$4,500 £2,000

One of a pair of large
George I octagonal tea
caddies, by E. Gibbon,
London, 1725, 21oz.
11dwt., 5¾in. high.
$5,065 £2,250

Set of three George III oblong
tea caddies in Chinese silver
mounted box. $10,800 £4,800

One of a pair of
George I tea caddies,
by F. Nelme, London,
1723, 44oz.
$12,600 £5,600

Silver tea caddy by Paul de
Lamerie, 1724, 13.3cm.
high, 15oz.13dwt.
$13,500 £6,000

One of three George II
tea caddies, by George
Methuen, London,
40oz.18dwt.
$13,500 £6,000

One of a pair of silver tea
caddies, by Paul de
Lamerie, London, 1751,
29oz.12dwt.
$22,500 £10,000

107

George III tea kettle, by
D. Smith and R. Sharp,
London, 1760.
$1,350 £600

George III tea kettle on
stand, 15¾in. high, by
John Edwards, London,
1792, 69oz.9dwt.
$1,400 £625

George II silver globular
tea kettle, stand and burner,
by Thos. Whipham, London,
1747, 61oz. $1,465 £650

George II tea kettle and
stand, by John Jacobs,
London, 1747.
$1,685 £750

George II tea kettle on
stand, 14½in. high, by
Peze Pilleau, London,
1755, 56oz.12dwt.
$2,025 £900

George II tea kettle on
stand, 13¼in. high overall,
by Christian Hillan, London,
1741, 51oz.17dwt.
$2,025 £900

George II tea kettle on stand,
15½in. high, by Gurney &
Cooke, London, 1758, 62oz.
19dwt. $2,140 £950

Early George III tea kettle
on stand, by Francis Crump,
London, 1769, 67oz.12dwt.,
15½in. high. $2,140 £950

George II silver tea kettle
on stand with burner, by
E. Wakelin, London, 1747,
76oz.12dwt., 14¾in. high.
$2,475 £1,100

George III tea kettle, by F. Butty and N. Dumee, London, 1766, 16in. high, 65oz.2dwt. $2,485 £1,100

George II pear-shaped tea kettle, stand and lamp, by Wm. Bagnall, 1759, 64oz. $2,585 £1,150

George II Irish tea kettle on lampstand, by John Taylor, 13in. high, 67oz.14dwt. $3,040 £1,350

George I tea kettle on stand, 14in. high, by John White, London, circa 1720, 73oz. 9dwt. $3,600 £1,600

Silver tea kettle, maker D. Smith and R. Sharp, London, 1761, 14in. high, 65oz. $3,600 £1,600

Early George II tea kettle on lampstand, by Thos. Tearle, London, 1728, 13½in. high, 80oz.17dwt.$7,200 £3,200

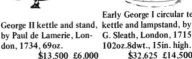

18th century Dutch tea kettle, 15¾in. high, 67oz.19dwt. $9,000 £4,000

George II kettle and stand, by Paul de Lamerie, London, 1734, 69oz. $13,500 £6,000

Early George I circular tea kettle and lampstand, by G. Sleath, London, 1715, 102oz.8dwt., 15in. high. $32,625 £14,500

TEAPOTS

George III shaped oval teapot, 6in. high, by Crispin Fuller, London, 1793, 15oz.6dwt. $865 £385

George III shaped oval teapot, 6in. high, London, 1789, 13oz.15dwt.
$945 £420

George II Scottish teapot, 6¾in. high, by Ebenezer Oliphant, Edinburgh, 1747, 22oz.1dwt. $1,015 £450

George III oval teapot, by John Denziloe, London, 1786, 15oz.1dwt., 5½in. high.
$1,070 £475

George III oval silver teapot, by Richard Sawyer, Dublin, 1799. $1,080 £480

George III 'Drum' teapot, by Makepeace and Carter, London, 1777, 4¼in. high, 13oz.14dwt. $1,125 £500

18th century Dutch pear-shaped teapot, by Jan de Vries, Amsterdam, 6in. high, 9oz.5dwt. $1,295 £575

George II pear-shaped teapot, 5½in. high, by Thos. Parr II, London, 1744, 15oz. 13dwt. $1,350 £600

George III shaped oval teapot, by Hester Bateman, London. 1787, 6in. high, 12oz. 18dwt. $1,350 £600

George II Scottish teapot, 6¾in. high, by Ker and Dempster, Edinburgh, 1754, 21oz.1dwt. $1,465 £650

George III oval teapot by Hester Bateman, 5½in. high, 13oz.1dwt. $1,485 £660

George III circular teapot and stand, circa 1770-73, London, 20oz.1dwt.
$1,520 £675

George II spherical teapot, by Johan Gothelf-Bilsings, Glasgow, circa 1745, 5¾in. high, 16oz.6dwt. $1,530 £680

George III 'Drum' teapot, by Parker & Wakelin, London, 1775, 5in. high, 15oz.10dwt. $1,575 £700

Silver teapot, by Peter and Anne Bateman, London, 1795, 20.5oz.
$1,800 £800

Silver teapot and stand, by Hester Bateman, 1787-89, 16cm. high, 16oz. $1,880 £835

George II bullet-shaped teapot, by Ayme Videau, 1741, 20oz. $1,920 £850

George III oval inverted pear-shaped teapot, by Wm. Dempster, Edinburgh, 6½in. high, 24oz.16dwt. $1,920 £850

Louis XVI cylindrical teapot, 4in. high, by Jacques Antoine Bonhomme, Paris, 1783, 12oz.11dwt. $2,195 £975

Early George II bullet-shaped teapot, 5½in. high, by John Main, Edinburgh, 1731, 20oz.16dwt. $2,250 £1,000

George I bullet-shaped teapot, by James Smith, London, 1719, 3¾in. high, 13oz. 9dwt. $2,925 £1,300

George II bullet-shaped teapot, by Richard Bayley, London, 1741, 14oz. 6dwt., 4½in. high. $3,040 £1,350

Mid 18th century Dutch plain teapot with stepped domed cover, 9oz.4dwt. $3,150 £1,400

George III octagonal teapot and stand, by Hester Bateman, London, 1787, 19oz.1dwt. $3,150 £1,400

18th century Dutch teapot, 6in. high, by Albert Giljaart, Haarlem, 1751, 8oz.12dwt. $3,375 £1,500

Early 18th century Flemish teapot, 4¼in. high. $3,375 £1,500

George I silver bullet-shaped teapot of plain design, by Fras. Helme, 11.5oz., London, 1724. $3,940 £1,750

George I bullet-shaped teapot, by Humphrey Payne, London, 1725, 5in. high, 14oz.2dwt.$4,500 £2,000

18th century Swiss teapot, 5¾in. high, 15oz.2dwt. $5,400 £2,400

18th century Dutch melon-shaped teapot, by Willem Langebeke, 10oz. 15dwt., 5¼in. high. $6,300 £2,800

Very rare Queen Anne silver teapot, by Gabriel Sleath, 1713. $7,200 £3,200

George I plain octagonal pear-shaped teapot, 1718, 16oz.19dwt.
          $11,700 £5,200

113

TOILET REQUISITES

Portuguese silver and stained fish-skin nécessaire de voyage, circa 1730-40. $1,295 £575

German oval toilet box, probably by Christian Winter or Christoph Warmberger, circa 1700, 8oz.12dwt.$2,925 £1,300

Charles II circular toilet box, 3½in. diam., London, 1683, 7oz.6dwt. $2,925 £1,300

George I spherical soap box, by E. Feline, London, 1721, 5oz.3dwt. $3,150 £1,400

Queen Anne toilet service, London, circa 1706, 81oz. 12dwt. $18,565 £8,250

Charles II toilet set, circa 1680, 158oz.
$49,500 £22,000

TONGS & NIPS

Feather edge tongs, maker I.H., circa 1775. $65 £30

Chased leaf tongs, by W. & J. Deane, London, circa 1765. $100 £45

Pair of sugar nips, by Wm. Penstone, London, circa 1774, 1oz., engraved with a crest. $125 £55

George III bright cut sugar tongs, by G. Smith and T. Hayter, London, 1798. $125 £55

Openwork tongs with acorn bowls, by Wm. Sheen, London, circa 1760.
$135 £60

Sugar tongs, by Hester Bateman, circa 1780. $225 £100

114

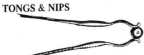

Silver asparagus tongs, by J. Buckett, of London, circa 1770, 23cm. long.
$225 £100

Irish silver nips with flower engraved box hinge, Dublin, 1765. $225 £100

Silver rococo period nips enhanced with gilding, 1745. $340 £150

Silver asparagus servers, by Thomas Northcote, 1790. $340 £150

Early 18th century silver sugar tongs, by L.E., London, circa 1710.
$730 £325

Rare pair of Irish provincial serving tongs, by Carden Terry, Cork, circa 1765, 5oz. $765 £340

TRAYS

George III oval tea tray, 22¼in. wide, by T. Renou, London, 1794, 64oz.5dwt.
$2,250 £1,000

George II shaped triangular tea kettle stand on hoof feet, by R. Abercrombie, 1735, 14oz. 11dwt. $3,600 £1,600

Late 17th century Dutch spice tray, Rotterdam, circa 1683, 8½in. wide, 5oz.15dwt.
$3,825 £1,700

George III two-handled tray, by J. Wakelin and R. Garrard, 1796, 80oz., 20in. long.
$5,175 £2,300

George III oval tea tray, 29in. overall, by T. Renou, London, 1796, 152oz. 10dwt. $5,625 £2,500

George III oval tea tray, by J. Crouch and T. Hannam, London, 1791, 14¼in. wide, 119oz.6dwt.$11,250 £5,000

One of a pair of George III boat-shaped sauce tureens and covers, 9in. wide, by Wm. Pitts, London, 1782, 41oz.3dwt.
$2,250 £1,000

One of a pair of George III silver gilt sauce tureens and covers, 11½in. wide, by J. Langlands and J. Robertson, Newcastle, 1788, 46oz.5dwt.
$2,590 £1,150

One of a pair of George III oval sauce tureens and covers, 9¼in. wide, by D. Smith and R. Sharp, London, 1778, 47oz.7dwt.
$2,815 £1,250

One of a pair of George III silver sauce tureens, by J. Carter, London, 1776, 45oz.
$3,035 £1,350

One of a pair of Louis XVI sauce tureens, 8in. wide, by H. Auguste, Paris, 1789, 35oz.12dwt. $4,050 £1,800

One of a pair of George III two-handled oval sauce tureens and covers, by Wm. Holmes, 1778, 43oz.
$4,500 £2,000

One of a pair of George III oval sauce tureens, by R. Hennell, 1777, 48oz.
$4,500 £2,000

One of a set of four George III sauce tureens and covers, by Paul Storr, London, 1797, 101oz.2dwt., 9in. wide overall.
$13,500 £6,000

Early George III oval soup tureen and cover, by John Vere and Wm. Lutwyche, London, 92oz.10dwt., 15¼in. wide.
$4,275 £1,900

George III oval soup tureen and cover, by T. Heming, London, 1776, 17¾in. wide, 84oz.4dwt. $7,650 £3,400

One of a pair of 18th century German small soup tureens and covers, 9½in. wide, circa 1730, 69oz.15dwt.
$7,875 £3,500

18th century soup tureen and cover, 17in. wide, by Johann Conrad Otersen, circa 1785, 111oz.12dwt.$10,125 £4,500

George II two-handled soup tureen and cover, Dublin 1745, 164oz., 13¾in. long. $11,250 £5,000

George III shaped oval soup tureen and cover, by Butty and Dumee, London, 1769, 16¾in. wide, 107oz.2dwt. $13,050 £5,800

Silver tureen and cover, by Bernhard Wilhelm Budde, Munster, circa 1763
$45,000 £20,000

French silver soup tureen, cover and stand, by Thomas Germain, Paris, one of a pair. $1,125,000 £500,000

117

George III tea urn , by F. Butty and N. Dumee, London, 1766, 19in. high, 73oz.10dwt. $1,520 £675

George III tea urn, by C. Wright, London, 1771, 80oz. $1,575 £700

Early 18th century Scottish urn, 11½in. high, Edinburgh, circa 1725, 43oz.11dwt. $1,855 £825

George III vase-shaped tea urn, 20in. high, by Parker and Wakelin, London, 1774, 89oz.8dwt. $2,025 £900

George III coffee urn. 14in. high, by D. Smith and R. Sharp, London, 1778, 24oz. 12dwt. $2,025 £900

George III oviform tea urn, by C. Wright, London, 1770, 79oz.11dwt., 20½in. high. $2,140 £950

George III tea urn, by C. Wright, London, 1771, 20½in. high, 70oz. $2,195 £975

George III vase-shaped tea urn, by Wakelin & Taylor, London, 1783, 77oz.3dwt., 18in. high. $2,250 £1,000

Early 18th century coffee urn, probably Flemish or Dutch colonial, 29oz.15dwt., 12¼in. high. $2,815 £1,250

George III silver tea urn, by Louisa Courtland, 1767, 25in. high. $3,375 £1,500

George III two-handled coffee urn, by E. Fernell, 1787, 47oz., 15in. high. $3,600 £1,600

George III vase-shaped tea urn, 22in. high, fully marked by Peter and Ann Bateman, London, 1796, 110oz.6dwt.$4,050 £1,800

George III vase-shaped tea urn, by J. Denziloe, London, 1789, 110oz.14dwt., 20½in. high. $4,275 £1,900

George III vase-shaped coffee urn, by Hester Bateman, London, 1783, 13½in. high, 35oz.17dwt. $4,500 £2,000

George III two-handled tea urn, by F. Butty and N. Dumee, 1768, 22½in. high. $4,725 £2,100

George III two-handled vase-shaped tea urn, by E. Fernell, 1787, 100oz., 23in. high. $4,950 £2,200

George III two-handled tea urn, by A. Fogelberg and S. Gilbert, 1780, 21¾in. high, 122oz. $6,300 £2,800

Unusual George II pear-shaped chocolate urn. $12,375 £5,500

119

George III sugar vase, by Robt. Hennell, London, 1784, 5in. high, 7oz.9dwt. $565 £250

George II baluster tea vase, 4¾in. high, by Peze Pilleau, 1747, 7oz. 15dwt. $1,015 £450

George III silver gilt covered vase, London, 1770, 20oz.6dwt., 8¼in. high. $1,125 £500

Late 18th century Austrian covered sugar vase, Vienna, 1794, 7½in. high, 17oz. 16dwt. $1,350 £600

One of two George III sweetmeat vases, by Robt. Hennell, London, 1781, 10oz.18dwt. $1,735 £770

18th century Maltese covered sugar vase, by Gio. Cassar, circa 1775, 6¼in. high, 11oz.17dwt. $2,025 £900

One of a set of three George III covered sugar vases, 9in. and 8in. high, by D. Smith and R. Sharp, London, 1785, 45oz.6dwt. $2,250 £1,000

One of a set of three George III sugar vases, by C. Makemeid, London, 1772, 26oz. 18dwt. $2,475 £1,100

One of a set of three George II sugar vases in sizes, by D. Piers, London, 1752, 43oz. 1dwt. $2,475 £1,100

George III rectangular vinaigrette, 1¼in. wide, by Thos. Holland, London, 1799. $270 £120

George III silver gilt vinaigrette, 1in. diam., by T. Phipps and E. Robinson, London, 1799. $350 £155

George III gold mounted agate vinaigrette, 1in. diam., circa 1780. $2,025 £900

WINE COOLERS

One of a pair of Sheffield plate wine coolers, circa 1790, 7in. high. $1,575 £700

George II wine cooler, by E. Wakelin, London, 1754, 65oz.5dwt. $8,440 £3,750

One of a pair of George III two-handled wine coolers, by R. and T. Makepeace, 1793, 162oz., 7½in. high. $10,125 £4,500

One of a pair of Catherine the Great wine coolers, by Z. Deichmann, 1766. $13,050 £5,800

One of a pair of George III silver gilt wine coolers, 10½in. high, 249oz.10dwt. $14,060 £6,250

One of four George III two-handled campana-shaped wine coolers, 10in. high, 407oz. $16,875 £7,500

George III oblong wine label, by Thos. Willmore, Birmingham. $100 £45

George III wine label, engraved for claret, by M. Binley, London, circa 1770. $125 £55

George III wine label, unmarked, circa 1790. $150 £65

George III reeded oblong wine label, by Susanna Parker, London, 1790. $190 £85

George II wine label for 'Cyder', maker's mark H.P., circa 1758. $215 £95

'Brandy' wine label, by Hester Bateman, circa 1775, 1¾in. wide. $260 £115

One of two George III crescent-shaped wine labels, by Hester Bateman, London, 1786-90. $295 £130

One of two cast wine labels in the mid 18th century style. $295 £130

One of two urn-shaped wine labels, by Phipps and Robinson, London, circa 1790. $315 £140

George III crescent-shaped wine label, by Hester Bateman, London, 1786-90. $395 £175

Rare 18th century wine label apparently unmarked, circa 1780. $585 £260

George III 'Madeira' wine label, by R.S., circa 1783. $1,485 £660

122

Silver wine funnel, circa 1775. $340 £150

George III silver wine funnel, London, 1778, 4¾in. high. $360 £160

George III funnel, by Thos. Graham, London, 1795, 4¼in. high, 1oz.4dwt. $610 £270

WINE TASTERS

18th century French silver wine taster. $305 £135

Early 18th century Scottish wine taster, 17dwt., 4¼in. wide. $325 £145

Early parcel gilt wine taster, 3½in. wide. $340 £150

Louis XVI silver wine taster, Paris, 1789, 3oz.10dwt. $870 £385

Charles II circular wine taster, 3¼in. diam., London, 1664, 1oz.18dwt. $1,400 £625

Mid 17th century wine taster, 4in. diam., 1oz.16dwt. $1,855 £825

Louis XV wine taster with shell thumbpiece, 3¼in. diam., circa 1740, 4oz.4dwt. $1,920 £850

William III wine taster, London 1695, 3oz.3dwt. $2,250 £1,000

Plain 17th century silver charka with engraved frieze, 3cm. high. $4,050 £1,800

INDEX

124